Charles Wesley's Verse

An Introduction

FRANK BAKER

Second Edition

EPWORTH PRESS

To the memory of
James Alan Kay

British Library Cataloguing in Publication Data

Baker, Frank, *1910*—
Charles Wesley's verse: an introduction.
—2nd ed.
1. Christian church. Public worship Hymns.
Words. Wesley, Charles, 1707–1788.
Critical studies
I. Title
264'.2'0924

ISBN 0–7162–0446–0

First edition published 1964
by Epworth Press
Second edition published 1988 by
Epworth Press
Room 195, 1 Central Buildings, London SW1H 9NR

Printed in Great Britain by
Richard Clay Ltd, Bungay, Suffolk

CONTENTS

PREFACE

I am happy to respond to the invitation of the Epworth Press to prepare a second edition of this work, first published twenty-five years ago as a lengthy introduction to my *Representative Verse of Charles Wesley*. During the last quarter of a century I have become even more familiar with the Wesleys, and have learned much more about the background of their publications. On the whole there seems little which needs changing in the volume, though I have added a chapter on early Methodist hymnology and have rewritten the chapter dealing with the problem of distinguishing between the hymns of the two younger Wesley brothers.

The major difference arising during this period, apart from many additional tributes to and studies of Charles Wesley, are the publication of a scholarly edition of John Wesley's own major hymn-book, and the preparation of a new ecumenical hymn-book by the Methodist Church.

A definitive edition of *A Collection of Hymns for the use of the People called Methodists*, published by John Wesley in 1780, has long been a desideratum for Wesley scholarship, ranked in Christian literature by a Congregational scholar with the Psalms, the Book of Common Prayer, and the Canon of the Mass, 'a work of supreme devotional art by a religious genius'. After long publishing delays this appeared in 1984, from The Clarendon Press of Oxford, though the title-page is dated 1983. In 1983 also appeared *Hymns and Psalms, A Methodist and Ecumenical Hymn Book*. This contains the irreplaceable nucleus of Wesley's *Collection*, varied and strengthened by much of the best of later hymn-writing, as chosen by representatives of almost all the denominations in the British Isles.

This second edition is greatly enriched by being able to refer to these rich resources for illustration of the thought and literary skills of Charles Wesley, in the year which marks the 250th anniversary of the spiritual awakening which unlocked the immense gifts of his devotional and lyrical genius.

Duke University,   Frank Baker
Durham, North Carolina
31 August 1987

1

The Discovery of Charles Wesley

There is little difficulty in securing enthusiastic tributes to the outstanding merits of Charles Wesley as a hymn-writer, even though these tributes are frequently tempered by the over-bold assertion that hymns cannot be poetry and the completely false assumption that Charles Wesley confined himself to hymns. Methodist admirers have waxed rhapsodical in his praise. As these may well be accused of partiality I refrain from quotation. Let the informed 'outsider' speak. It was a cautious Unitarian, Dr Alexander Gordon, who thus described Charles Wesley's hymns: 'Rich in melody, they invite to singing, and in the best of them there is a lyrical swing and an undertone of mystical fervour which both vitalize and mellow the substratum of doctrine.'[1] It was a shrewd and scholarly Congregational layman, Bernard Lord Manning, who claimed that the 1780 *Collection of Hymns for the use of the People called Methodists* — almost pure Charles Wesley — 'ranks in Christian literature with the Psalms, the Book of Common Prayer, the Canon of the Mass. In its own way it is perfect, un-approachable, elemental in its perfection. You cannot alter it except to mar it; it is a work of supreme devotional art by a religious genius.'[2] And it was an Anglican, Dr John Julian, outlining the hymnological contribution of

the Wesley family for his monumental *Dictionary of Hymnology*, who placed the bardic wreath on his head: 'But, after
all, it was Charles Wesley who was the *great* hymn-writer of
the Wesley family — perhaps, taking quantity and quality
into consideration, the great hymn-writer of all ages.'

Since the time of Stopford Brooke's *Theology in the English
Poets* (1874) there has been a growing awareness of Charles
Wesley's important place in the history of English verse in
general, an awareness accompanied by a recognition of
the fact that hymns even of a quality far lower than his
average compositions play an essential part both in the
development of literary taste and in the shaping of literary
achievement. Certainly Charles Wesley's competence as a
verse-writer has increasingly been recognized, and pro-
fessors of English literature have come to agree with John
Wesley that in the compositions of his brother there are
to be found not only 'the purity, the strength, and the
elegance of the English language', but in some of them 'the
true spirit of poetry'.[3] Edmund Gosse acknowledged that
'the sacred songs of Charles Wesley ... reach at their
noblest the highest level of Protestant religious poetry
in this country since George Herbert'.[4] W. J. Courthope
described him as 'the most admirable *devotional* lyric
poet in the English language'.[5] George Saintsbury treated
Wesley as the leader of the small group of truly inspired
writers of religious verse who in the eighteenth century
became 'more positively poetical than most of the profane'.[6]
Oliver Elton placed him 'at the head of all English hymnologists', illustrating the statement that he 'often attains
to poetry, and is much oftener on the brink of it' by
references to his 'verbal music and easily rememberable
sound', his 'ringing vowels', and his ear for rhythm, which
'often keeps the hymn going when the language flags'.[7]

From the quotations so far presented it is obvious that
Charles Wesley already fills an important niche in the

history of English poetry. The magnitude of his achievement, however, has been opening up to students of English literature in general only during the last two or three decades, and even now there is a vast hinterland waiting to be explored. Although a revered Methodist professor, Dr Henry Bett, had for over a generation been proclaiming the literary riches to be found in Wesley's hymns, their real discovery by the world of letters may be traced to the writings of Bernard L. Manning, quoted above, and to those of George Sampson, particularly his Warton Lecture on English Poetry, delivered before the British Academy in 1943. Under the title 'A Century of Divine Songs' Mr Sampson outlined the contribution made to English literature during the eighteenth century by the hymn — 'the poor man's poetry' and 'the ordinary man's theology'. Taking as his (unannounced) text George Saintsbury's dictum quoted above, Mr Sampson claimed that eighteenth-century hymns — particularly those of the Wesleys, to whom over half the lecture is devoted — constituted a far more important literary achievement than any contemporary secular verse, and that they 'helped to form the very texture of the English mind'. And yet, he complained, 'this extraordinary outburst of religious poetry is ignored in most histories of English literature as if it had never existed'.

The pronouncements of Mr Manning and Mr Sampson compelled students of our literature to pay more attention to the work of hymn-writers, and particularly to the verse of Charles Wesley, the greatest of them all. Among other studies that of Dr Donald Davie — *Purity of Diction in English Verse* (1952) — may be noted as an important contribution to the theory of poetry. Dr Davie takes Charles Wesley as the first major example of a restrained classicism in verse which achieves its effects not through luxuriant metaphor but through 'purity of diction'. This is no sign

of literary poverty, but of artistic economy in words and
metaphors. Dr Davie illustrates the wide range of Wesley's
language, his power in wielding simple words, the sophisti-
cation of his verse structure, his skilful use of the *dénouement* in the closing line, his wealth of allusion, and his
ability to resuscitate a dead metaphor. It can safely be
prophesied that the exploration of Charles Wesley's vast
contribution to English literature will continue to increase,
and will continually unearth new treasures.

Manning's high tribute to John Wesley's 1780 *Collection*
of the classical hymns of the Methodist movement (quoted
above) can at last be tested by the reader. Early in 1984
(though it bears the date 1983) The Clarendon Press,
Oxford, published a scholarly illustrated edition of its 525
hymns in 848 pages, with considerable attention to its
sources, its tunes, and its theology, as well as its text and its
history as the major general hymn-book for Methodists.
Charles Wesley was far and away its chief author, but the
selection, arrangement, and editing were that of his older
brother John, and it appeared as Volume 7 of the Oxford /
Bicentennial Edition of his Works. It will frequently be
referred to below as *Collection*, without the qualifying date.

In the same year of 1983 the British Methodist Church
published a new successor as general hymn-book, *Hymns
and Psalms, A Methodist and Ecumenical Hymn Book*. Not
only were Methodists involved in its preparation, but
'members of the Baptist Union, Churches of Christ, Church
of England, Congregational Federation, and the United
Reformed Church'. Henceforth the regular source for
consulting Wesley hymns may be regarded as this volume
rather than *The Methodist Hymn Book* of 1933, even though
that volume does contain upwards of eighty more of their
hymns.

In this work the primary source of reference for quotations will be the *Collection*, because of its more traditional

text and fuller documentation. Failing that we use *Hymns and Psalms*. In some instances both are in some way defective for our specific purposes, especially in representing the complete original text. In these instances we refer to the work for which this introduction was first prepared, *Representative Verse of Charles Wesley*, using the form, *Rep. Verse*, 54:15–17, and/or p. 73.

2

Charles Wesley's Literary Output

One of the major problems facing any student of Charles Wesley's verse is that of his enormous literary output. The hundreds of his hymns in the older Wesleyan hymn-books are only small selections; the thirteen volumes of his *Poetical Works* omit over thirteen hundred poems available only in manuscript. Even a widely representative collection such as that for which this introduction was written is quite inadequate for the research student who seeks to do more than acquire the basic 'feel' of Wesley's writing. It is well at the outset to understand something of the magnitude of the task of even *reading* all Wesley's verse, let alone studying it.

Many have smiled over George Saintsbury's characteristic dictum: 'They say Charles Wesley wrote between six and seven thousand hymns — a sin of excess for which he perhaps deserved a very short sojourn in the mildest shades of Purgatory, before his translation upwards for the best of them.'[1] Actually this fabulous figure is both understatement and overstatement. It is an exaggeration to speak of six thousand 'hymns' if that term is to be used in a narrowly specific sense, as defined below; it is a serious understatement if by 'hymn' we mean — as most people who make such statements about Charles Wesley's writings usually do mean — his verse compositions as a whole, or even those with more or less religious content.

I dare not claim that my own statistics contain no element of error — the task of compilation is beset with multifarious problems — but the figure of 8,990 of his poems which I have read is near enough to nine thousand to proclaim that 'round' number as the total of his extant poems *as he left them*. The last cautionary phrase is necessary because of the many alterations to which they have been subjected, division into separate parts here, combination of smaller units into a larger unit there, and extracts everywhere. In particular it is fairly common knowledge that many of his compositions were (to use his own description) 'Short Hymns' of only one or two stanzas. To gain an adequate understanding of the scope of his literary output, therefore, it is necessary to count the lines, not the poems. To summarize the results of such a wearying though (I believe) necessary undertaking, we may take it that Charles Wesley wrote (again in round figures) nine thousand poems, containing 27,000 stanzas and 180,000 lines. This is something like three times the output of one of our most prolific poets, William Wordsworth, and even more than that of the redoubtable Robert Browning. Moreover, unlike both these poets, Charles Wesley's verse consists almost solely of lyrics in stanzaic form — a mere 7,500 lines are extant in various couplet forms. Taking the average — and it must be stressed that this is an *average*, not a description of normal practice — Charles Wesley wrote ten lines of verse every day for fifty years, completing an extant poem every other day.

Much has been written about the dangers of facility in verse, and most of it applies to Charles Wesley. He left scores of poems incomplete — many of them published in that form without any hint that the author had originally intended an addition or continuation. There are hundreds that he could have improved, should have improved, and almost certainly would have improved had he deliberately prepared them for publication. Oliver Elton's comment contains much truth, though it is far from being the whole truth: 'Charles Wesley has the note of the *improvisatore*, with whom it is hit or miss ... He goes wrong, not through over-elaboration, but through neglect of finish.' For the defence we can produce thousands of poems which Charles Wesley carefully revised time and time again, particularly the 3,500 manuscript poems on the Gospels and the Acts, whose five volumes were worked through and touched up eight times between their completion in 1764 and his death in 1788. His extant manuscripts abound in erasures, alterations, and alternative words — as may be seen in some of the texts and collations in *Representative Verse of Charles Wesley*. Even these frequently revised poems, however, often betray signs that they were originally composed in the saddle rather than in the study, and are more memorable for their flow and pace than for their depth or their polish.[2] Many a poem came to him white-hot, and its original casting has only been tampered with to its detriment. It cannot even be said that all Charles Wesley's own revisions were obvious improvements, though this is more nearly true of the editorial emendations of his brother John.

In his *Life of the Rev. John Wesley* Henry Moore preserves an interesting picture of 'brother Charles' at work on his verse from youth to age: 'When at the University, in early youth, his brother (as he informed me) was alarmed whenever [Charles] entered his study. *Aut insanit homo, aut versus facit*.[3] Full of the muse, and being shortsighted, he would sometimes walk right against his brother's table, and, perhaps, overthrow it. If the "fine phrenzy" was not quite so high, he would discompose the books and papers in the study, ask some questions without always waiting for a reply, repeat some poetry that just then struck him, and at length leave his brother to his regularity ... When he was nearly fourscore, he retained something of this eccentricity. He rode every day (clothed for winter even in summer) a little horse, grey with age. When he mounted, if a subject struck him, he proceeded to expand, and put it in order. He would write a hymn thus given him on a card (kept for the purpose) with his pencil, in shorthand. Not infrequently he has come to our house in the City-road,[4] and, having left the poney in the *garden* in front, he would enter, crying out, "Pen and ink! Pen and ink!" These being supplied, he wrote the hymn he had been composing. When this was done, he would look round on those present, and salute them with much kindness, ask after their health, give out a short hymn, and thus put all in mind of eternity.'[5]

This emphasizes the fact that Wesley's poetic inspiration continued into old age. He had translated Latin classics into competent couplets in his youth and early maturity, at least during the decade of his twenties, but his lyrical genius was not kindled until his conversion in 1738, after which he poured out spiritual lyrics — some left unfinished — for half a century. We are sometimes tempted to think that he burned himself out during the first decade following his conversion, but this is far from the truth. The last five years of his literary career (1784–88) produced almost exactly as much as the first, over three hundred poems, though few of them were published. Over the fifty years there had been some comparatively barren stretches, but there was only one quinquennium when he did not write over a hundred poems. During one phenomenal five-year period (1762–66) he wrote no fewer than 6,248 scriptural hymns — an average of 1,250 a year! Nor is this marvel much diminished because many of these were 'short hymns' of one or two stanzas on individual verses or phrases, and it is

certainly heightened by the fact that the general quality
remained very high. Many poems published during his
fifties were as memorable as any penned during his thirties.
Nevertheless he continued to touch up his manuscript
volumes of scriptural hymns, 'completed' 1763–66, but
given seven thorough revisions between 1774 and 1787.
Even as he passed eighty he did not lose his touch, witness
his last poem, dictated to his wife as he returned from 'an
airing in a coach' a few days before his death:

> In age and feebleness extreme,
> Who shall a helpless worm redeem?
> Jesus, my only hope thou art,
> Strength of my failing flesh and heart.
> O could I catch a smile from thee
> And drop into eternity!

3

Classical Training

Between those two pictures of the poet at work, as an
Oxford tutor in his early twenties and as a veteran Anglican
clergyman and Methodist preacher on the verge of eighty,
there is much more than a gulf of fifty years' literary
experience — there is a complete transformation, both
in content, in form, and in inspiration. Yet it must be
claimed that the academic exercises and experiments of
the student of Christ Church, Oxford, his myopic absorp-
tion in the classics, and especially in the Latin poets, tilled
the soil for what became his life's blossoming. It has usually
been assumed that Charles Wesley suddenly became a poet
at his conversion in 1738, that 'Where shall my wond'ring
soul begin?' was, in fact, his first substantial venture into
verse. Nothing could be farther from the truth, although
this assertion is not susceptible of absolute proof. He was
already, I am convinced, a matured poet. Already he had
written hundreds of competent versifications of the classics
in the manner of Dryden or Pope. This seems to have
been a major preoccupation of his nine years at Oxford,
the foundation having been laid by thirteen years at
Westminster School under his elder brother Samuel, himself a noteworthy classicist and poet, as was their father
before them. At Westminster Charles Wesley had become
saturated with the classics of Greece and Rome as he was
later to become saturated with the classics of Samaria and

Jerusalem. In both cases his enthusiasm found expression
in a series of occasional poems inspired by his meditations
on purple passages. His *Short Hymns on Select Passages of the
Holy Scriptures* and his five subsequent volumes on the
Gospels and the Acts have survived. His youthful volumes
on the classics have disappeared, and only fragments
remain.[1] Those fragments, however, form a reminder of
the deep classical scholarship and of the genuine poetical
talent displayed while he was still an Oxford don. Doubtless he dreamed of an academic future when he would
gather the heady literary fruits of his solid classical studies
at Westminster and Oxford. He did reap his harvest, but it
was not the kind that he had expected.

Any full understanding of the verse of Charles Wesley
must begin with this classical background, and with an
educational system that insisted on aspects of literary study
which are now regarded as unimportant sidelines if not the
veriest eccentricities. In Wesley's youth the swing in higher
education towards mathematics and modern languages was
only in its infancy. The classics still held the field, together
with the arts of thinking, of writing, and of speaking,
which went with them. Rhetoric, in particular, which we
hardly consider a basic academic subject, was then a most
important part of education both at grammar school and
university level, and those strange 'exercises' before
graduation at Oxford and Cambridge were largely modelled
on the practice of the Schools of Rhetoric organized in
Athens by Marcus Aurelius. The study of rhetoric was
essential to the matter, as well as to the manner, of the 'acts'
and 'opponencies' at Oxford, and colleges offered prizes
for 'declamations'. This was the academic atmosphere in
which both Wesleys breathed freely. In their days there
were no examinations in 'practical' or 'applied' subjects,
and their mother tongue was almost a foreign language.
All was 'pure' and as far removed from the realities of

daily living as dead languages could make it. Even though there were symptoms of academic decay at Oxford, and although the mediaeval system was on its way out, one of the basic elements of the Methodist reformation at the university was a revival of learning as well as of religion, and of learning moulded on traditional classical lines. The classics continued to provide genuine inspiration to both Wesleys, and when John Wesley founded his own grammar school at Kingswood it was on classical lines. Vossius' *Rhetoric* was prescribed as a text-book for the senior class, whose pupils had to 'learn to make themes and declaim'.

The picture may seem slightly overdrawn, but at least it should serve to underline the fact that Charles Wesley's art of versification was quite consciously an *art*, and a carefully practised art, long before he was fired with religious inspiration. When we refer to rhetorical devices in his verse, devices with fearsome titles such as anadiplosis and aposiopesis, chiasmus, epizeuxis, oxymoron, and parison, it is no perversity of the enthusiastic researcher who imagines minutiae which don't really exist, and thus makes the process of Charles Wesley's verse-making sound much more complicated than it really was. Nor is it that Wesley had accidentally stumbled upon a way of saying things which had a peculiar structure and therefore a peculiar literary effect. It was all there in his classical training, a training so thorough that the vocabulary, the style, and the structure of his verse were markedly affected by it. This is not to suggest, of course, that every rhetorical device, every Latinism or metrical effect, was deliberately thought out by Wesley, any more than they are by other poets. But a particular mode of writing, the classical mode, had become so ingrained that even when he wrote unpremeditated verse some of its features frequently recalled the classical tutor's study almost as much as the prayer-room or the pulpit.

As experiences accumulated for Charles Wesley with the passing of the busy years — ordination, travel, 'heart-warming', evangelical preaching, marriage, family joys and anxieties, deep concern over the pattern of contemporary church life, political shocks — the young Oxford tutor developed out of all recognition. His verse gained new notes, experimented with new techniques, acquired a new depth — and height. Gradually the Bible came to mean to him even more than the classics had meant, saturating his language in speech and in verse. Yet the scriptures never completely ousted the classics, either in thought or in composition — witness the quotations from Horace and Virgil and Ovid prefixed to the political verse of his seventies.[2] They remained parallel streams watering the broad and fertile acres of his post-conversion years.

4

The Spiritual Impetus

Although the beginnings of his capacity for the making of
memorable verses must be sought in his classical training,
the name of Charles Wesley could hardly have been known
and loved in millions of homes across two centuries and
five continents apart from the quickening of his talent
through a spiritual impetus. For any great poetry to be
written there must be both consummate craftsmanship
and a powerful urge. Without the spiritual urge that was
born at Whitsuntide 1738 and that continued through
varying phases to his life's end, Charles Wesley would have
been both more and less successful as a poet than in fact
he became. He would (I believe) almost certainly have
achieved widespread recognition as a minor poet, possibly
as one of the major poets; he would have written some
really great love poems (always assuming that he had fallen
in love!) and he would have made a name chiefly by his
scintillating satire — a more polished Butler or Swift, a
more virile companion for Gray, Goldsmith and Collins.
He would have been admired, feted and feared in the
literary circles of his own day, and applauded by the literary
historians of every day. This did not happen, however,
and it is of course impossible to prove that it would have
happened. In the event his talents as a poet were both
enriched and engulfed by his discovery of a rapturous
personal religion. Henceforth all other activities, no matter

how deeply felt, how vividly expressed in verse at the
time, assumed but secondary importance compared with
his spiritual obsession. This spiritual obsession brought a
new note into English secular verse and swelled immeasur-
ably the rising tide of hymnody — hymnody which over-
flowed into sacred poetry and became a formative influence
in the literary education of the average Englishman.

Both Charles Wesley's chief strength and the main reason
for the comparative neglect of his verse by literary students
are to be found in the basic content of his published work.
In his day it was considered 'enthusiastic' to undergo deep
religious emotion, and most indecorous to *write* about
such matters. Yet the Wesleys and their followers undoubtedly did experience deep religious emotions, just as they
thought deeply upon theological problems (which was
socially permissible), and they became convinced that the
conventional inhibitions and reticences about personal
religion were at least partly to blame for the cold frustra-
tions of the century. Therefore they must broadcast the
good news of personal salvation from sin through faith
in the Lord Jesus Christ, the normality of a personal assurance of that saving faith, and the possibility of the crowning spiritual experience of what was variously called
'holiness', 'Christian perfection', or 'perfect love'.

The Wesleys were profoundly convinced that a personal
experience of God's saving and sustaining love was possible
not only for an elect few, but for all men. In their theological thought they went to the very brink of Calvinism,
endorsing its emphasis upon the sovereignty of God, but
then drew back. Salvation must be 'free', but it must also be
'for all', otherwise it was hardly a gospel. Both became key-
notes of Methodist preaching and Methodist singing. The
theological atmosphere of English religion was changed
from the rigid Calvinism of the seventeenth century to the
Arminianism and modified Calvinism of the nineteenth

century. In this theological revolution no two men played a greater part than the brothers Wesley, and it seems likely that the hymns of Charles were even more influential than the sermons of John.

This gospel, illustrated from scripture, from theological debate, and from personal experience, formed the one theme of Charles Wesley's hymns. When Dr J.E. Rattenbury wrote on *The Evangelical Doctrines of Charles Wesley's Hymns* there was no implication that any other doctrines were of central importance to Wesley. Everything else was bent to this: the ventures into the Arminian-Calvinist controversy, the more academic verse on the doctrine of the Holy Trinity, the mysticism and sacramentarianism of the *Hymns on the Lord's Supper,* nearly every paraphrase and meditation based on the Old Testament as well as on the New — all was seen through the gospel glow, every event was brought to its focus in the cross, the divine act on behalf of man. Even Wesley's love poems needed only a few light touches to transform them into hymns; even his poems of spiritual despair have a substratum of assurance; hardly a topical or a controversial or a political poem but eventually leads to the cross and to the final crown in heaven. Charles Wesley did write poems, many more poems than has generally been realized, which were not strongly tinctured with the glowing colours of his own deep faith — but he did not publish them. His published work was a weapon of his evangelism, both in creating the atmosphere and in reinforcing the message of the Methodist preacher. Indeed in some respects the exhortation from the pulpit was a far less effective weapon than the song in the pew.

The subsequent lowering of the spiritual temperature, even within Methodism, made it somewhat difficult after a few generations to sing many of Charles Wesley's greatest hymns without either hypocrisy or at least a faintly uneasy self-consciousness — a 'defect' from which the hymns of Isaac Watts do not suffer, for they enshrine, not the heights and depths of the human soul, but 'average religious sentiment'.[1] One example of this debasing of Wesley's spiritual currency is to be seen in his preoccupation with heaven. One of the most characteristic features of his hymns is the way in which, no matter with what earthly subject they begin, they end in heaven. Not only a clear belief in an after-life, but frequent and fervent thoughts about it were common both to saint and sinner in Wesley's day. Death as the entrance to this after-life obtruded itself much more upon the attention of adults and children alike then than now — quite apart from the fact of a much higher rate of mortality. Gradually agnosticism has laid its cold hand on the man in the street, and even the man in the pew neither wishes to be reminded too frequently about death nor has very clear views about heaven or about hell. As a result our hymn-books have required drastic revision. Many hymns, such as 'Ah! lovely appearance of death!', and only in 1983 'Rejoice for a brother deceased' — have been completely banished. Others have been truncated by the omission of the closing references to heaven. Yet heaven for Charles Wesley was not simply a place of rest — or even of joy — after death. Heaven was a relationship between God and man, a relationship summed up in the word 'love', just as the person of Christ was summed up as 'Love', and just as the perfect life of the Christian was summed up as 'love'. In other words, heaven was in some sense present in the Christian's earthly communion with God, and the real heavenliness of the after-life was the enlargement and enrichment of this communion. This is seen constantly in Charles Wesley's poems, including the excised portions, as in this final stanza (omitted from the hymn-books) of his 'O for a thousand tongues':

> With me, your chief [i.e. chief of sinners],
>   you then shall *know*,
> Shall feel your sins forgiven;
> Anticipate your heaven below,
>   And own, that love is Heaven.[2]

Not only did Wesley's conversion introduce him to depths and heights of personal emotion. Not only did it help him to view those emotions in the context of eternity. It also enlarged the boundaries of his experience horizontally upon earth as well as vertically into heaven, by making him more susceptible to the emotions of others. Nor is 'susceptible' a large enough word; he was more responsive to the emotions of others, deeply, desperately concerned about them, for they were the potential children of God, and lived on the threshold of eternity. So powerful was the sympathetic link between Charles Wesley and others that it is sometimes exceedingly difficult to be sure whether in his verse he is describing his own experience or identifying himself with that of someone else. Occasionally clues of time or place or circumstance make it clear that he writes of himself. In other instances it is just as clear that he is thinking and feeling himself into the personality of another, as when he writes for wives and widows, coal-miners and criminals, lay preachers, Loyalist soldiers, or the scholars at Kingswood School. There remains a large body of verse, however, where — unless new evidence is forthcoming, such as is occasionally available in his manu-scripts — it is impossible to be sure whether he portrays personal or vicarious experience. Dr Rattenbury pointed out that his use of the first person singular is often 'a piece of dramatic personation', as when he writes:

> Pity my simplicity,
> Suffer me to come to Thee.

On the other hand Dr Rattenbury also stressed the fact
that the penitential hymns in the first person are usually
far more powerful and convincing than those in the third
person, and are therefore the more likely to have emerged
from Wesley's own experience. Be that so, his faculty of
convincing 'personation' remains. There is little doubt
that Charles Wesley's personal discovery of religious faith
brought such an intensifying of sensitivity that his identification with the emotions of others led to the development
in his verse of what can justly be described as a form of
dramatic art. 'It is in this dramatic poetry, combining
liturgy and evangelism,' says Mr T. S. Gregory, 'that we
can discern the genius of Charles Wesley'.[3]

5

Charles Wesley's Vocabulary

Having thus sketched in the academic and spiritual background to Charles Wesley's ventures into verse, it is desirable to analyse some of the literary characteristics of his
work, and thus to demonstrate in some small way the
manner in which his heritage was transmuted into genuine
poetic achievement. Dr Donald Davie claims that Wesley
takes a Latin word and 'refurbishes' it so that 'the blunted
meaning or the buried metaphor comes sharp and live
again, by a sort of Latinate pun'.[1] Dr Henry Bett gives
many examples of such words — 'expressed' (a shape
struck out with a die), 'illustrate' (illuminate), 'secure' (free
from care), 'tremendous' (terrifying), 'virtue' (manliness
or power).[2] Most of these words have suffered from continuous debasement, so that it is difficult to recapture the
shade of meaning which they had for Wesley, and in some
cases wellnigh impossible without a footnote. The word
'pompous', for instance, recalled the due dignity of a
magnificent procession without any of its modern over-
tones of ostentation.

Wesley displayed a Miltonic facility for incorporating
polysyllabic Latinate words into the texture of his verse in
such a manner that they illustrated his theme, introduced a
modulation into the verbal music, and varied without dis-
rupting the rhythm. Adjectives and adverbs ending in
'-able, -ably' and '-ible, -ibly' were particular favourites, but

nouns and verbs were used with similar effect. A well-
known and deservedly praised example is found in the
opening stanza of one of his *Nativity Hymns*:

> Let earth and heaven combine,
>   Angels and men agree
> To praise in songs divine
>   Th' incarnate deity,
> Our God contracted to a span,
> Incomprehensibly made man.

This illustrates what Dr Davie describes as the threading
of Latinisms on the staple Anglo-Saxon of his diction so
that both 'criss-cross and light up each the other's meaning'
— witness, 'songs/divine', 'contracted/span', and 'incom-
prehensibly/man'. Moreover every word is used precisely,
not only (as we shall see later) carefully chosen and carefully placed, but so carefully chosen and placed that clear
thought about its exact meaning is demanded of the reader,
and always rewarded. Wesley's is the art of the etcher,
sharp and definite rather than vague and suggestive.

   Some people are basically afraid of precision and pro-
fundity in hymns, and are also apt to confuse a lengthy
word with prolixity. An interesting example is to be found
in 'O Thou who camest from above'. Wesley wrote of the
'flame of sacred love' kindled on the altar of his heart:

> There let it for thy glory burn
> With inextinguishable blaze.

This was too much for the compilers of the ill-fated 1904
edition of *Hymns Ancient and Modern*, who replaced classical
tautness by tautology, making the second line read 'with
ever-bright, undying blaze.' This meddlesome botch (as
John Wesley would undoubtedly have called it) did not
find its way into the 'standard edition' of *Hymns Ancient and
Modern*, and was happily refused entry to the 1950 edition,

which restored a few other of Wesley's original readings. Unfortunately, however, as Mr Findlay pointed out,[3] it was retained in the BBC *Hymn Book*.

It must be granted that Wesley's introduction of Latinisms in order to point and illustrate his thought does not always 'come off', mainly because he is writing above our heads. Most of us lag far behind him in our familiarity with the classics. It needs, therefore, not only a mental effort, but the consultation of a lexicon, in order to appreciate fully some of his words and phrases. We are in much the position of the rank and file of Wesley's converts: we get the gist of his thought through the sturdy Anglo-Saxon, and are swept past the finer points of the Latin allusion. Unlike most sermon-tasters, we understand the argument, but not the illustration. A few familiar examples may be quoted, prefaced by the warning that because they are familiar we may miss their fuller significance:

> Blest with this antepast of heaven![4]

> Still present with Thy people Thou
> Bear'st them thro' life's disparted wave.[5]

> Unmark'd by human eye,
> The latent Godhead lay.[6]

> Concentred all thro' Jesus' name
> In perfect harmony.[7]

Greek words are nothing like so frequent in Wesley's verse as those from ancient Rome, and they almost always come from the Greek of the New Testament. A familiar example is the use of 'panoply' — the original is πανοπλία — in 'Soldiers of Christ, arise'. Another occurs in a favourite stanza of both Dr Bett and Mr Manning, taken from one of Wesley's *Hymns Occasioned by the Earthquake* (1750), where he describes the unshaken house awaiting the Christian in the City of God:

> Those amaranthine bowers,
>   Inalienably ours,
> Bloom, our infinite reward,
>   Rise, our permanent abode,
> From the founded world prepared,
>   Purchased by the blood of God.

Both Bett and Manning point out the Latinism of 'founded' and the retention of the original Greek in the musical 'amaranthine'. I may add the point that this latter retention is quite deliberate, for the English translation 'never-fading' would have fitted the metre equally well.[8]

Very occasionally there are references to or reminiscences of the Hebrew text of the Old Testament. In some stanzas on Isaiah 9.6–7, 'The mighty God, the everlasting Father', Wesley prefixes the normal translation of the Authorized Version, but in the poem itself instead of 'everlasting Father' uses the literal translation from the Hebrew, 'Father of eternity'. Similarly, in the phrase from Psalm 8.5 about man being made 'a little lower than the angels' he prefers the original (which is followed by the Revised Version), and reads ' a little lower than God', somewhat to the consternation of the non-Hebraists among the Methodists.[9]

When all has been said, however, it must be reasserted that the basic texture of Wesley's speech was provided by Anglo-Saxon, in which every now and then was woven a bright pattern of classical words. Wesley's Anglo-Saxon was derived (like that of many of our greatest writers) from the King James Version of the Bible. This was partly because Bible words and phrases permeated the atmosphere that he breathed as a boy at Epworth, and partly because the solid purity of their diction appealed to his clean, direct mind. Even his pre-conversion translations from the classics are more Anglo-Saxon than Latin in their vocabulary. Certainly after his conversion he deliberately chose homespun words, both because they formed the language of the English Bible and because they spoke most clearly to the ordinary man. Although Wesley is occasionally Miltonic in his use of the sonorous Latin word, in general he is much more akin to his distant kinsman Daniel Defoe in his use of robust though rarely colloquial common speech. Charles Wesley's Latinisms generally enforce and illustrate for the educated man the basic meaning conveyed in staple Anglo-Saxon to the less erudite worshipper. The deliberate Latinisms, therefore, are comparatively few, though always significant.

This predominant use of the mother tongue was the more noteworthy in an era of neo-classicism, when scholars were fond of larding their weighty tomes with Greek and Latin quotations. John and Charles Wesley sometimes used Latin and Greek in conversation and in correspondence for the sake of privacy or precision, and knew as many classical tags as the next Master of Arts, but both carefully refrained from any form of classical ostentation. Just as their volumes were reduced in size, so their sentences were freed from superfluity and ambiguity for the sake of the 'man in the street'. They wrote plain English for plain people. This economy in words was the result in part of training, in part of a purified taste, and in part of deliberate restraint for the purposes of evangelism. The result both in prose and in verse was a lucid, direct, forceful style whose influence on the spread of Methodism, as even on English literature, was greater than has often been recognized.

Moreover, Anglo-Saxon is direct and monosyllabic compared with the elaborations and profundities of Latin and Greek. Words derived from Anglo-Saxon are therefore likely to be more vigorous than those from the classical languages, whose strength lies in the ability to express a finer precision of thought. The one is more appropriate for action, the other for contemplation. For the most part Charles Welsey's verse is not mystical nor quietly contemplative; certainly it does not embody an eager pursuit of knowledge for its own sake. The note of wonder and awe is never far away, but primarily Wesley's hymns are poems of action — of theological action, the action of God in Christ, matched by the responding action of man.[10]

This marriage of common speech to the timeless realities of personal religion, rather than the jargon of the *literati* harnessed to the latest academic or scientific fashion, almost preserves Wesley from the charge of being 'dated'. Almost but not quite. His verse contains a few less happy Latinisms and some archaic grammatical constructions. He frequently introduces ideas distasteful to modern congregations, such as 'bowels', 'blood', and 'worms' — though the criticism here must be levelled at the Bible rather than at the eighteenth century.[11] Nevertheless there is surely much truth in Dr Bett's claim that Wesley's vocabulary is 'distinctly the most modern diction to be found in eighteenth-century verse',[12] and in Mr George Sampson's comment in his Warton lecture that the language of the common man for which Wordsworth sought so painfully, because the belles-lettres of the eighteenth century merely echoed the *patois* of the drawing-room, was nevertheless enshrined in verse in the hymns of the Evangelical Revival. In some of these hymns — as in those of John Cennick — it was used at its most colloquial or with the exaggerated technicalities and sentimentalities of contemporary piety at its worst, but in those of Charles Wesley it was normally purified and strengthened, rarely stilted or erudite.

Nevertheless Charles Wesley was not afraid to experiment with unusual terms, particularly with lengthened and strengthened forms of common words, even though they involved the wedding of Anglo-Saxon and Latin. Some such terms were already available for him, though they might be archaic. Such was 'implunge', used in his brief but exhilarating response to the invitation of Revelation 22.17 'And let him that is athirst come', where nothing but the biggest words would do for the rapturous climax:

> Thy call I exult to obey,
>   And come in the spirit of prayer,
> Thy joy in that happiest day,
>   Thy kingdom of glory to share;
> To drink the pure river of bliss,
>   With life everlasting o'erflow'd,
> Implung'd in the chrystal abyss,
>   And lost in an ocean of God![13]

Occasionally he would coin a word. One very interesting example, not noted in the *Oxford English Dictonary*, occurs in a well-known poem, but has been almost lost through carelessness or timidity or a combination of both. The early manuscripts and printed editions of 'Soldiers of Christ, arise' show that Wesley originally wrote:

> Extend the arms of mighty prayer,
>   Ingrasping all mankind.

He could perfectly well have used 'embracing' except that its sentimental connotations might have cheapened the climax. On the other hand in his day it would have been possible to use 'grasp' as a synonym, though the normal meaning was 'to inclose in the hand, to take hold on with the hand, to seize on'.[14] He set aside the conventional term for a bold adaptation of the word that by itself did not quite fit. His coined 'ingrasping' is both robust and also creates a vigorous mental picture of the mighty arms of prayer spreading wide enough to clasp all men within their embrace. In face of the orthodoxy of printers, however, combined with the obstinacy of most who read or sang the

hymn, he seems eventually to have acquiesced in the split-
ting of this powerful coining into its two components.[15]

Whether derived from Anglo-Saxon, Latin, Greek, or
Hebrew, from a combination of two of them, or springing
from his own eager mind, Charles Wesley constantly
sought *le mot juste*. Hence the hundreds of variant readings
in his manuscripts. A case in point is the hymn that John
Wesley and a midlands congregation were singing at the
moment of Charles Wesley's death — 'Come let us join our
friends above', whose fourth stanza closed:

> Ev'n now by faith we join our hands
>   With those that went before,
> And greet the blood-besprinkled bands
>   On the eternal shore.

Two manuscripts are available for this hymn. In one a
blank has been left, and 'blood-besprinkled' fitted later
into that blank. In the other the same line receives still
further attention, 'greet' being struck through and replaced in the margin by 'grasp', which in its turn gives way
to 'clasp'. Finally 'greet' is reinstated.[16] Perhaps more striking is the choice of a word in a poem prepared by Wesley
for his pregnant wife in 1755, intended as a prayer for her
use in the coming ordeal:

> Who so near the birth hast brought,
>   (Since I on Thee rely)
> Tell me, Saviour, wilt thou not
>   Thy farther help supply?
> Whisper to my list'ning soul,
>   Wilt thou not my strength renew,
> Nature's fears and pangs control,
>   And bring thy handmaid through?

In the fifth line Wesley originally wrote 'Speak it to
my list'ning soul', which means almost the same, but

unhesitatingly discarded this for the music and mystery of 'whisper', with its reminiscence of the powerful presence of God made known to Elijah in the 'still small voice', to which he refers in his *Scripture Hymns* as 'the soft whispering voice of love'.[17]

Dr Oliver Beckerlegge has greatly enriched our understanding of Charles Wesley's imaginative and forceful use of unusual words by a series of commentaries on a select group of them, varying from Latinism to archaism to neologism.[18] They include actuate, antedate, consentaneous, deprecate, displicence, effectuate, engross, impending, incumbent, inspoken, meeken, obtest, sensualize, tendered, ungrasp, upstarting. One of the remarkable things about his verse is how what seems a most unlikely word somehow comes alive within a particular context.

As a tribute to Charles Wesley's precision, flexibility, and economy in the use of words, we can do no better than to quote John Wesley's preface to the 1780 *Collection*, remembering that this statement applies chiefly to his brother's verse, which makes up the bulk of the volume: 'In these hymns there is no doggerel, no botches, nothing put in to patch up the rhyme, no feeble expletives. Here is nothing turgid or bombast on the one hand, nor low and creeping on the other.[19] Here are no *cant* expressions, no words without meaning ... Here are (allow me to say) both the purity, the strength, and the elegance of the English language — and at the same time the utmost simplicity and plainness, suited to every capacity.' This tribute, of course, covers far more than the vocabulary, but summarizes also the style, or the use made of that vocabulary, to which we now turn.

6

Literary Allusions

One of the delights of reading is to be moving in two dimensions at the same time — in the dimension of the immediate reality of the story being told or the theme being expounded, and also in the dimension of allusions, which light up different aspects of the subject from the viewpoint of other writings or experiences, and thus make it vital and vivid. As in his vocabulary so in his literary illustrations Charles Wesley drew from wide reading, but again primarily from the Bible. We have already seen that he often used single words from Latin and Greek as metaphors in miniature. Sometimes this allusive quality of his verse extends to a phrase, a sentence, or even several sentences. Dr Bett shows how a famous passage in the *Aeneid* (vi. 724–9) colours one of Wesley's poems — 'Author of every work divine' — and also draws attention to the influence both of Horace and of Edward Young on another — 'Stand th'omnipotent decree' Bett suggests that Horace's 'Caelum, non animum mutant, qui trans mare currunt', recalled either consciously or unconsciously, was the probable origin of some striking lines in one of the *Hymns occasioned by the Earthquake, March 8, 1750:*

> In vain ye change your place,
>   If still unchanged your mind:
> Or fly to distant climes, unless
>   Ye leave your sins behind.

There is a possible allusion to the *Iliad* (viii. 19) in the 'golden chains' of 'Author of every work divine,' noted above, and a more sustained reference in one of the *Hymns for the Nativity of our Lord*, 'Join all ye joyful nations'. Here Wesley alludes to the Greek legend of Hercules strangling in his cradle the snakes sent to destroy him, a legend typically translated into the Christian idiom, though this particular stanza was marked by John Wesley for future omission:

> Gaze on that helpless object
> Of endless adoration!
>   Those infant hands
>   Shall burst our bands,
> And work out our salvation;
> Strangle the crooked serpent,
> Destroy his works for ever,
>   And open set
>   The heavenly gate
> To every true believer.[1]

Dr Bett also garners echoes in Charles Wesley's verse of several English poets, particularly Shakespeare, Milton, Herbert, Dryden, Pope, Prior, and Young.[2] It is almost inevitable that the phraseology of a man's favourite authors should find their way, sometimes unnoticed, into his own writings, though the results in the case of Charles Wesley are occasionally quite surprising to the modern reader. Most of us are familiar with the fact that 'Love divine, all loves excelling' follows the stanzaic pattern as well as echoes the opening words of Dryden's 'Fairest Isle', but very few of us would realize unaided the debt of 'Jesu, Lover of my soul' to Prior's *Solomon*, in its direct quotation of the phrase 'the nearer waters roll'. Undoubtedly this is a direct quotation, for *Solomon* was a favourite poem with both John and Charles Wesley; it occupies a hundred

pages of John's *Collection of Moral and Sacred Poems*,[3]
and Charles urged his daughter Sally to memorize it completely![4] Another familiar echo of Prior's *Solomon* is to
be found in the closing lines of 'Christ, from whom all
blessings flow':

> Love, like death, hath all destroyed,
> Rendered all distinctions void:
> Names, and sects, and parties fall;
> Thou, O Christ, art all in all!

A glance at Prior's own lines makes the debt unmistakable:

> Or grant thy passion has these names destroy'd:
> That Love, like Death, makes all distinction void.

Charles Wesley's elder brother Samuel also influenced
him greatly, and that not only by teaching him to appreciate and practise the compressed, balanced, epigrammatic
verse modelled on the classics. Constant reminiscences of
Samuel's own poems appear in those of Charles. Dr Bett
points out some of them, including the striking allusions in
'Christ the Lord is risen today' to Samuel's 'Hymn on
Easter Day', part of which ran:

> In vain the stone, the watch, the seal,
>   Forbid an early rise,
> To Him who breaks the gates of hell,
>   And opens Paradise.

Dr Bett demonstrates the debt by printing in italics the
borrowed phrases in the better-known hymn by Charles:

> *Vain the stone, the watch, the seal,*
> Christ hath *burst the gates of hell*:
> Death *in vain forbids His rise,*
> Christ hath *opened Paradise*![5]

Strangely enough Dr Bett omits to mention that one
of Charles Wesley's most telling phrases — 'Our God

contracted to a span', from 'Let earth and heaven combine'
— quotes the last four words of Samuel Wesley's 'Hymn to
God the Son', though he does point out its more remote
possible ancestry, 'contract into a span' used in a quite
different context in George Herbert's 'The Pulley'.[6]

Once more, however, it is the Bible that provides Wesley
with a never-failing source of allusions as of matter and of
language. A detailed familiarity with the scriptures was
the 'extra poetic dimension' (to use Dr Davie's phrase) in
which Wesley could move at will and be fairly certain that
others could follow him, both the more educated among
his readers and, — to some extent at least, — the few
among the Methodist worshippers who remained illiterate.[7]
Through the scripture-saturated hymns of Charles Wesley
Bible-reading and hymn-singing were mutually enriched.

Much has already been written about the wealth of scriptural allusions in Wesley's hymns, and undoubtedly much
more will yet be written. There is no need to labour the
point, but two illustrations may be given. In Wesley's day it
was quite unnecessary to expound to a Methodist congregation the closing lines of 'Sing to the great Jehovah's
praise', which are usually omitted from modern hymn-
books either because of their theology of the Second
Advent or because of the misleading Latinate construction
in the second line. As so often, the hymn ends in heaven,
with the Second Coming of our Lord, but this is illustrated
by a doubled metaphor from the Old Testament:

> 'Till Jesus in the clouds appear
>   To saints on earth forgiven,
> And bring the grand sabbatic year,
>   The jubilee of heaven.

More subtle is the way in which Charles Wesley equates his
conversion with the Spirit of God brooding over the face of
the waters when the earth was without form and void
(Genesis 1.2):

> Long o'er my formless soul
> The dreary waves did roll;
> Void I lay and sunk in night:
> Thou, the overshadowing Dove,
> Call'dst the chaos into light,
> Bad'st me be, and live, and love.[8]

Even the Bible commentators are echoed in Wesley's verse. Dr Bett notes his allusions to Luther on Galatians in 'O Filial Deity', as also his use of Bengel. The Rev. A. Kingsley Lloyd and Dr Erik Routley have demonstrated Wesley's indebtedness to the better-known commentary of Matthew Henry in 'Wrestling Jacob', 'Captain of Israel's Host', 'A charge to keep', and other poems.[9] Allusions to the Primitive Fathers, the liturgies, and the mystics are also pointed out by Dr Bett.[10] If, however, we were to add all the allusions and quotations from all the commentators and Christian writers through the centuries as a supplement to all those from the poets, philosophers, and historians both classical and modern (supposing that this were in fact possible) it seems clear that they would be but as a drop in a bucket beside Wesley's use of the scriptures. This is the vast ocean from which he draws. His verse is an enormous sponge filled to saturation with Bible words, Bible similes, Bible metaphors, Bible stories, Bible themes. In the thirty-two lines of 'With glorious clouds encompassed round' Dr W. F. Moulton found references to no fewer than fifty verses of scripture.[11] In preparing the annotated 1780 *Collection* a plethora of scriptural allusions threatened to swamp the editors, so that only those which gained positive threefold approval from Hildebrandt, Beckerlegge, and Baker were admitted, in strict application of the rule, 'When in doubt, throw it out.' Nevertheless the Index of Scriptural Allusions occupies pp. 807–34! Indeed, in the memorable words of Dr J. E. Rattenbury, 'A skilful man, if the Bible were lost, might extract much of it from Wesley's hymns. They contain the Bible in solution.'[12]

7

The Art of Rhetoric

Wesley's classical background was of some importance, as we have seen, in his choice of vocabulary and his employment of allusion. It was far more important, however, indeed it was a dominant factor, in the more artificial (a better word might be 'artistic') elements of his style: the subtle or startling changes in the normal usage of words, the careful arrangement of both words and ideas so as to bring richer meaning by parallels or contrasts or sequences, or even by somewhat complicated interlockings, and particularly by the many changes rung on the art of repetition. Most of this artistic use of words is so skilful that it is only noticed when pointed out, yet it is the secret of Charles Wesley's most characteristic effect, the compact tautness of his verse, the epigrammatic intensity, as if a powerful steel spring had been compressed into his lines, so that they were always trying to burst their restraints. This is by no means true of all his poems, but it is true of a far greater number than might be generally recognized. In some few of them the spring (to continue the metaphor) has been allowed to shoot out and quiver at its full extent. Or, to change the metaphor, some poems give the effect of a spate of words tumbling over one another, or of a smoothly flowing stream, rather than of a huge weight of water dammed up so that a mere fraction spurts through under terrific pressure. Wesley's anapaestic verses

almost uniformly afford examples of rapid unimpeded
flow.

It must be insisted that this effect of the restrained
energy of a coiled spring or a dammed stream, both in its
general intention and in its particular application, was
deliberate, though there may well be scores and hundreds
of undesigned examples. Wesley's style was consciously
moulded on that of the ancient classics, and he copied
many or most of their rhetorical devices. Not that he
was constantly saying to himself, 'Now we must have an
oxymoron here, and a chiasmus there', or 'Here at last is a
good opportunity for an aposiopesis!' By the time Charles
Wesley came to write his greatest poems he was thirty years
old, and nearly twenty years of close application to classical
studies had made this literary discipline an integral part
of his mental processes, just as an experienced preacher
almost unconsciously analyses his ideas into 'points'. The
appreciation, the terminology, and the practice of rhetoric
had become almost as essential an element of his approach
to literature as his A B C. Willy-nilly he worked that way —
and working that way was one of the chief reasons for his
success.

The Art of Rhetoric was a common title for text-books
which helped the schoolboys and undergraduates of the
sixteenth, seventeenth, and eighteenth centuries to choose
and marshal their words, both in speech and writing,
with the fullest effect. There were over three hundred
different terms by which they could describe the 'tropes'
and 'figures' and 'fine turns' used by the ancients to make
language clear, forceful, and beautiful. The peak period
for the use of these devices in English was probably the late
sixteenth century, about the time of Puttenham's *Arte of
Poesie*, which describes over a hundred of them. Gradually
the art of rhetoric was transmuted from the poet's dream
to the schoolboy's nightmare, and eventually faded into

the light of common day, becoming a memory and an aroma difficult for men of our scientific era to recapture. Even after the middle of the eighteenth century, however, the rhetoricians, though fewer, were far from extinct. In 1755 a grammar school master named John Holmes published an *Art of Rhetoric* listing over two hundred and fifty rhetorical terms with explanations and illustrative examples. Some of these terms have found their way into common speech — words such as enigma, irony, sarcasm. More survive as technical terms still used by grammarians — like apostrophe, ellipsis, euphemism, periphrasis, and even hyperbole, synecdoche, and prolepsis. Others are almost completely forgotten.

In defence of *The Art of Rhetoric* it should be pointed out that technical terms have great importance in simplifying the complications of life. It is therefore a serious mistake to assign more than its value as satire to the words of one of Wesley's favourite poems, Butler's *Hudibras*:

> For all a Rhetorician's Rules
> Teach nothing but to name his Tools.

This displays excellent rhetoric — in the unfortunate derogatory sense of that word — but poor intelligence. For it *is* important, as any surgeon would insist, to know the names as well as the uses of one's tools. It is a great economy of time and effort if a single word can be used instead of an involved description, possibly supported by an illustrative example. Yet many of the Greek, Latin, or Latinized Greek terms which were the rhetorician's tools have not found their way even into the larger dictionaries. Granted that some of them had synonyms, and that others were too finicky to be of permanent value; nevertheless not all those laid aside were useless or cumbersome. How, for instance, would we describe a long succession of sub-ordinate clauses whose meaning is at last made clear by the

completion of the sentence? A good example is 'If ..., if
..., if ..., if ... — You'll be a man, my son!' It hardly seems
satisfactory to define this as 'the rhetorical device that
forms the basis of Kipling's "If".' But 'the Greeks had a
word for it' — a word which was adopted by the Romans,
and which came into English with the rest of the para-
phernalia of rhetoric, but has now been thrown out as
lumber. The word was 'hirmos' or 'hirmus', which is
not even to be found in the monumental *Oxford English
Dictionary*. Many other terms, for figures of thought or
speech which are much more complicated, have no place
in our larger dictionaries. We therefore tend to overlook
the fact that these were among the commonplaces of
literary appreciation and practice in past centuries. It will
not be possible here to do more than name a few of the
more common rhetorical devices by which Wesley trans-
mitted both energy and polish to his verse.

To follow Holmes's *Art of Rhetoric*, there were three main
classes of such devices — tropes, figures, and 'fine turns'.
He lists seven main tropes, or 'saying one thing and
meaning another': metaphor, its extension the allegory,
metonymy, synecdoche, irony, hyperbole, and catachresis.
In describing each principal trope he mentions other
minor ones associated with them, and goes on to refer to
other devices sometimes classed as tropes. This abnormal
usage of words in order to convey a vivid mental image is,
of course, basic to the creative vision of peotry, and many
interesting examples can be found in Wesley, whereby he
gives poetic force to abstract statements. Sometimes this
is in single phrases such as 'our inward Eden'.[1] At other
times Wesley uses a more fully developed metaphor, as
when he describes the Incarnation of our Lord in terms
of undressing and dressing, a metaphor dignified, as well
as somewhat disguised, by his use of slightly uncommon
words:

> He laid his glory by,
>   He wrapped him in our clay.[2]

The same poem furnishes an example of one of his favourite sea-going metaphors of 'sounding the depths':

> See in that Infant's face
>   The depths of deity,
> And labour while ye gaze
>   To sound the mystery.[3]

This occurs in much simpler form in 'Come, Holy Ghost, our hearts inspire' which ends:

> And sound, with all Thy saints below,
>   The depths of Love Divine.

Although on occasion Charles Wesley mixed his metaphors or at least passed too rapidly from one to another, we find many examples of carefully sustained metaphors which almost become allegorical. Such is that in 'Rejoice for a brother deceased':

> Our brother the haven hath gained,
>   Out-flying the tempest and wind...
>
> And left his companions behind;
> Still tossed on a sea of distress,
>   Hard toiling to make the blest shore...
>
> There all the ship's company meet,
>   Who sailed with the Saviour beneath...
>
> The voyage of life's at an end.[4]

Metaphor is undoubtedly the most important of the 'tropes' used by Wesley as by most poets, though examples of other tropes constantly occur. For instance there is the antonomasia of 'Come all ye Magdalens in lust' in 'Where shall my wond'ring soul begin', where a proper noun is used as a general epithet;[5] there is the synecdoche of 'The mournful, broken hearts rejoice' in 'O for a thousand tongues', where a part is used instead of the whole; and there is the somewhat annoying metonymy of speaking about 'the stony' instead of 'the stony heart', as in 'Sinners, obey the Gospel word'.[6] Hyperbole is a favourite device, as in the soaring anapaestics portraying the ecstasies of conversion, for which no ordinary language is sufficient:

> I rode on the sky
> (Freely justified I!)
> Nor envied Elijah his seat;
> My soul mounted higher
> In a chariot of fire,
> And the moon it was under my feet.[7]

John Holmes lists twenty 'principal and most moving figures in speech' and many more either related to these, or unrelated but of only minor importance, to which he adds the terms brought over into rhetoric from grammar and logic. Again a few examples must suffice. It is by now a commonplace to point out Wesley's use of exclamation mark: — ecphonesis, to use the rhetorician's term. It was impossible to confine the rapture of the Christian experience of God to a mere statement of fact, and sometimes it could only be expressed (and quite imperfectly at that) by a series of exclamatory phrases which had ceased to form part of a normal sentence. A good example, even though the actual punctuation marks are mainly commas, is to be found in the closing four stanzas of 'Sinners, obey the Gospel word'. The invitation in stanza six to accept 'the plenitude of gospel grace' is followed by a series of nineteen phrases suggesting varied aspects of the regenerate life, which tumble over one another so rapidly that they have the force of a series of exclamations rather than the elaborations of a prior statement:

> A pardon written with His blood,
> The favour and the peace of God,
> The seeing eye, the feeling sense,
> The mystic joy of penitence;
>
> The godly grief, the pleasing smart,
> The meltings of a broken heart,
> The tears that speak your sins forgiv'n,
> The sighs that waft your soul to heav'n.
>
> The guiltless shame, the sweet distress,
> Th'unutterable tenderness,
> The genuine meek humility,
> The wonder, why such love to me!
>
> Th'o'erwhelming pow'r of saving grace,
> The sight that veils the seraph's face,
> The speechless awe that dares not move,
> And all the silent heaven of love![8]

The device of hypotyposis or 'lively description' serves to bring a scene immediately before our eyes, as in Wesley's 'Hymn for Ascension Day' ('Hail the day that sees Him rise'):

> See! He lifts his hands above!
> See! He shews the prints of love!
> Hark! His gracious lips bestow
> Blessings on his church below!

Wesley's parentheses are often masterly:

> He left his Father's throne above,
>   (So free, so infinite his grace!)
> Emptied himself of all but love,
>   And bled for Adam's helpless race.[9]

One of his favourite mannerisms in this category is to paint a damning generalized picture of sin — or of God's forgiving grace — and then to bring himself into the picture in a dramatic final parenthesis. In 'Where shall my wond'ring soul begin' the sixth stanza generally offers salvation to harlots and murderers, and closes 'He died for crimes like yours — and mine.'[10] Wesley can even make a periphrasis add energy to his lines instead of obscuring and weakening them, though he is very sparing in his use of circumlocutions, preferring direct phrases. In the much-discussed 'Ah! lovely appearance of death' he pictures the powdered, rouged, and bedizened ladies of fashion, contrasting them very unfavourably with the bare and seemingly brutal simplicity of death:

> Not all the gay pageants that breathe
> Can with a dead body compare.[11]

Perhaps the sentiment no longer commands our admiration, but we can still feel (when we realize what he's about) the force of the contrast between the deliberately elaborate periphrasis of 'the gay pageants that breathe' and the directness of 'a dead body'.

Figures of thought and speech involving a contrast held a particular attraction for Charles Wesley, or perhaps we should say that only thus could he approach an adequate expression of the basic paradoxes of the Christian faith. Simple contrasts of ideas, or antitheses, are woven into most of his verse. Sometimes they are obvious and normal, as that between the verbs and the nouns in:

> Raise the fallen, cheer the faint,
> Heal the sick, and lead the blind.[12]

Often they are much more subtle. 'How happy are the little flock', one of the *Hymns for the Year 1756*, furnishes several examples. The opening lines of stanza 3 contain a simple statement:

> The plague, and dearth, and din of war
> Our Saviour's swift approach declare,
>   And bid our hearts arise.[13]

The following three lines continue the same theme, with the 1755 earthquakes as the subject this time, but with far more subtlety:

> Earth's basis shook confirms our hope,
> Its cities' fall but lifts us up,
>   To meet Thee in the skies.

The contrast between the physical fall of the city and the spiritual rise of the Christian soul is on quite a different level from 'Raise the fallen, cheer the faint', and the other antithesis may very well have been missed, namely that between 'shook' (then grammatically acceptable for 'shaken') and 'confirms', which still retained something of the physical solidity of its original Latin meaning, and was certainly so used here by Wesley. The following stanza repeats the claim that these cataclysmic events foreshadow the Second Advent of Christ, and encloses within the statement antithetical demonstrations from the four calamities already listed:

> Thy tokens we with joy confess,
> The war proclaims the Prince of Peace,
>   The earthquake speaks thy power,
> The famine all thy fulness brings,
> The plague presents thy healing wings,
>   And nature's final hour.[14]

Occasionally such antitheses are practically indistinguishable from paradox:

> Dead is all the life they live,
>   Dark their light, while void of thee.[15]

The pure paradox or self-contradiction is also to be found, as in 'Jesus, the first and last':

> Yet when the work is done,
> The work is but begun.[16]

The antithesis also shades off into the oxymoron or combination for special effects of words which seem to be contradictory. Many examples could be given, from 'the guiltless shame, the sweet distress' of the regenerate experience quoted above, and 'Wrestling Jacob's' 'confident in self-despair', to 'their humbled Lord' and 'th'invisible appears' of 'Glory be to God on high'. Some would limit the term oxymoron to 'adjective + noun' or 'adverb + adjective', as in 'Victim divine' and 'death divine'[17] or — a phrase which describes the strange blend of opposites to be found in his own verse — 'I want a calmly-fervent zeal'.[18] It may bear the wider connotation, however, and so can be applied to antitheses pushed to the nth degree, as in 'Impassive, He suffers; Immortal, He dies.'[19] Whatever terminology is used the terse vigour and imaginative power of such phrases cannot be gainsaid. And once again it is the supreme mysteries of the Incarnation and the Atonement which constantly demand expression in this way — for how can an Eternal Being either be born or die? Typical of Wesley's approach in the *Nativity Hymns* is the couplet in 'Glory be to God on high':

> Being's Source *begins to* be,
> And God himself is *born!*[20]

In many ways the most interesting group of Wesley's rhetorical devices comprises those classed by Holmes as 'fine turns', in other words the various types of repetition. These not only add strength and vigour to individual phrases, but also serve to bind together both lines and stanzas. Holmes names fourteen 'chief repetitions', and adds eight minor types. One of the simplest forms is common to most poets, namely anaphora, or the repetition of the same word at the beginning of consecutive phrases or sentences, or (in the case of poetry) lines. One example from Wesley must suffice:

> Enough for all, enough for each,
> Enough for evermore.[21]

The immediate repetition of a word or phrase within the same sentence, or epizeuxis, is another common method of securing emphasis, as in 'Who for me, for me hast died'.[22] Less common generally, but frequent in Wesley, is epanadiplosis, beginning and ending a clause or line with the same word, as in 'Come, Desire of nations, come',[23] 'Hide me, O my Saviour hide',[24] and one from the funeral hymn 'Happy soul, thy days are ended':

> Go, by angel-guards attended,
> To the sight of Jesus go![25]

Repetition of a word or words at the end of lines or phrases is known as epistrophe. A good example is the opening stanza of 'Free Grace':

> And can it be, that I should gain
>   An interest in the Saviour's blood!
> Died He for me? — who caused his pain!
>   For me? — who him to death pursued.
> Amazing love! how can it be
> That thou, my God, shouldst die for me?[26]

It will be noticed that the phrase 'for me', although in each case it comes at the end of a phrase — indeed in the second instance it constitutes the complete phrase — is actually introduced in three different positions in the line, and only comes at the end when it is most needed for emphasis, in the very last line. One reason is that Wesley (like his father

before him, *vide* his *Essay on Poetry*) knew the dangers of
double rhymes, except in humorous verse. The other, and
chief reason, is that Wesley used subtlety in his repetitions,
so that they knocked at the back door of the subconscious
mind, and gained admittance without the master of the
house always being aware of how the divine visitation had
occurred. Even more subtle is the effect of wonder created
in the same stanza by the mesodiplosis or repetition of the
phrase 'can it be' in the middle of successive sentences,
once near the beginning of a line and once at the end, first
with the note of questioning predominant and then with
the note of awed astonishment at something that really has
happened.

Another less common device popular with Wesley is that
of using the last word or phrase of one clause as the first
of the following, thus securing both the emphasis of an
important point and the continuity of the argument:

> Earnest thou of joys divine,
> Joys divine on me bestowed.[27]

This echoing of an announced theme is very useful as a
means of binding stanzas together, as may be seen in the
closing and opening lines of stanzas 3 and 4 of 'The Love-
Feast' ('Come, and let us sweetly join'):

> We our dying Lord confess,
> We are Jesu's witnesses.
>
> Witnesses that Christ hath died,
> We with him are crucified.[28]

People have racked their brains to find a descriptive title
for this feature of Wesley's verse. Mr Findlay (who has
garnered seventy examples from the 1876 *Collection*) uses
what he agrees is the 'rather obscure heading' of 'last and
first words'.[29] Wesley himself knew the name of this

most useful rhetorical tool, and we need not be ashamed
of using it — or rather them — after him. The alternative technical terms for this device are anadiplosis and
epanastrophe.

The rhetoricians distinguished several less obvious
forms of repetition, but we will mention only three more.
The repetition of a phrase in reverse order was known as
antistrophe. It occurs in a number of Wesley's well-known
hymns, as in 'Thine to ours, and ours to thine',[30] and
constantly forced itself upon him in his Trinitarian verse
— 'One in Three, and Three in One' or 'Three in One,
and One in Three'.[31] (The corresponding pattern in
thoughts rather than words is chiasmus, mentioned below.)
Ringing the changes on different forms of the same word
was known by the Latin term *traductio*, an example of
which is found in 'For the Anniversary Day of One's Conversion', from which 'O for a thousand tongues' is extracted:

> My second, real, living life
> I then began to live.[32]

Familiar to all writers of verse, of good and especially
of bad, is the other device of repetition which we shall
mention, the refrain or (as the rhetoricians termed it)
epimone. Wesley's use of the refrain really demands an
essay in itself. He uses it in strict moderation, knowing how
easily a refrain can become forced or feeble, or the cloak
for poverty of thought or craftsmanship. Wesley's are
always strong phrases which readily stand up to repetition
in a prominent position, though they are often movingly
simple, like that to 'O Love Divine, what hast Thou done?'
which is an adaptation from Ignatius' *Epistle to the Romans* –
– 'My Lord, my Love is crucified'.[33] He never allows a
refrain to be repeated too frequently, as may well be seen
from the variations of the last line in 'Wrestling Jacob'.[34]
And he is adept at transforming a strong refrain into an

even stronger climax. A good example is 'Rejoice, the Lord is king', whose opening word is taken up in the refrain:

> Lift up your heart, lift up your voice,
> Rejoice, again I say, rejoice.

We notice how this refrain is itself consolidated by the balanced phrases with their anaphora in the first line, and by the epanadiplosis in the second line, in which he simply follows another orator trained in the schools of rhetoric, St Paul.[35] After five such refrains the poem is rounded off with a new couplet that takes us from earth to heaven but finishes on that same trumpet-word with which the poem began, an extended epanadiplosis:

> We soon shall hear th'archangel's voice,
> The trump of God shall sound, Rejoice.[36]

So far we have looked at fairly straightforward examples of the basic types of 'fine turns' or repetition. With an ear as sensitive and a mind as resourceful as Charles Wesley's, however, the real mastery is shown in the combination of such devices, and in their extension to other devices which have as yet been given no name. 'For the Anniversary Day of One's Conversion' echoes Luther's comment on St Paul, which meant so much in the deepened spiritual experiences both of John and Charles Wesley. We see not only the ringing of the changes on *me* and *my* (traductio), and the powerful wrenching of the correct grammatical order of the words (anastrophe) in order to underline the marvel of God's doing that for *him*; there is also a modified anaphora and a double epizeuxis:

> I felt my Lord's atoning blood
>   Close to *my* soul applied;
> *Me, me* he loved — the Son of God
>   For *me*, for *me* He died![37]

Wesley's anaphora itself is frequently, we might almost say usually, accompanied by a subtle change, not only in the word-music, but in the meaning also. It is not *mere* repetition but repetition with a difference, or — as the Greeks and the rhetoricians termed it — antanaclasis. Here is an example combined with antistrophe. The last line of stanza 8 of 'Christ the Lord is ris'n today' runs 'Hid our life with Christ in God!' Most of these words are repeated in the first line of the following stanza: 'Hid; till Christ our life appear'. Not only is the sequence of words changed, however — a completely new meaning is given to the phrase 'our life', which in the first instance has a human, in the second a divine, connotation.[38] Many similar examples could be quoted where an echo is combined with a slight change both in words and meaning, as in 'Jesu, Lover of my soul':

> All my trust on thee is stayed;
> All my help from thee I bring.[39]

Here the change is from passive to active, from rest to movement. Again in 'Father, whose everlasting love':

> We all *must* own that God is true;
> We all *may* feel, that God is love.[40]

Here the shift within the basic repetition is from universal compulsion to individual choice. This is a frequent sequence of thought with Wesley — 'For all the fallen race — and me!'[41]

One very interesting feature of Wesley's repetitions is a progression by which several words of one line are taken up and extended in the following line — a kind of enlarged and extended anadiplosis which might perhaps be termed epiploce. Stanza 2 of 'God of unexampled grace' ends 'Was never love like thine!' This is taken up in the opening line of stanza 3, with the addition of the term 'sorrow' and the amplification of 'thine':

> Never love nor sorrow was
> Like that my Jesus showed.[42]

Often the patterns of repetition are interlaced in such a way that it is almost impossible to notice them all at a first reading, though all have their unrealized impact. A good example is furnished by the closing stanza from 'O Love Divine, how sweet thou art':

> Thy only love do I require
> Nothing on earth beneath desire,
>   Nothing in heaven above:
> Let earth and heaven, and all things go,
> Give me thine only love to know,
>   Give me thine only love.[43]

The bold repetition of all but the last two words of the fifth line as the closing line strikes immediately. We realize on examination that the whole stanza furnishes an example of epanadiplosis, the same phrase being used for the beginning and the end — with the slight variation of 'thy' to 'thine'. Then we see that Charles Wesley has also contrived to give us an intermediate stage by using that same key phrase 'thine only love' in the very middle of the penultimate line, just as it is at the beginning of the opening line and the closing of the last line. Then, perhaps, we notice the anaphora of 'Nothing ...Nothing', linked in turn with the antithetical 'earth beneath' and 'heaven above', which are then gathered together in one phrase, 'earth and heaven'.

This latter device of accumulating single ideas for summarizing as a compound unity is paralleled by the more frequently employed reverse procedure — announcing the compound idea first, and then developing separately each component. An example of this is provided in 'Come on, my partners in distress', where the closing lines of the first stanza read:

> And look beyond the vale of tears
>   To that celestial hill.

The verb and preposition are each taken up (in reverse order) and expanded in the opening lines of the following stanza:

> Beyond the bounds of time, and space,
> Look forward to that happy place,
>   The saints' secure abode.[44]

When (as often) Charles Wesley wants to emphasize the universality of Christ's saviourhood, he keeps hammering the word 'all' and the phrase 'for all' into our minds, yet with all his insistence contrives to vary his theme so skilfully that the reader or singer does not fully realize how his subconscious mind is being bombarded. (Let us call this, as does Holmes, 'tautotes', and reserve 'tautology' for clumsiness in repetition, which Wesley's is certainly not.) In 'Let earth and heaven agree' stanza 6 introduces the theme quietly:

> For me, and all mankind,
>   The Lamb of God was slain ...
> Loving to all, he none pass'd by ...

(In passing we note that the 'all' is in fact implicit in the closing negative clause.) Stanza 7 ends on the same note: 'What thou for all mankind hast done!' Stanza 8 repeats the word 'all' in the second syllable of each of the last three lines, but in each case with a different word of introduction:

> For this alone I breathe
>   To spread the gospel-sound,
> Glad tidings of thy death
>   To all the nations round;
> Who all *may* feel thy blood applied,
> Since all are freely justified.

At last in stanza 9, before the quiet closing 'amen' of stanza
10, the full battery is brought into play, taking up the
simple second syllable 'all' in the second line (with yet
another introductory word) and letting it expand into an
emphatic 'for all' (introduced in stanza 7) at the end of
the fourth line. The phrase is hammered home at the
beginning of the following line, and for good measure
there is a two-fold repetition to open the last line:

> O for a trumpet-voice,
>   On all the world to call,
> To bid their hearts rejoice
>   In him, who died for all!
> For all, my Lord was crucified,
> For all, for all my Saviour died.[45]

The devices of repetition crowd one upon another —
tautotes, anadiplosis, anaphora, epizeuxis. Yet though the
effect is there and is strongly felt, we are conscious of no
straining after effect. Indeed it is hard to realize that just
over half of the last fifteen words consist of 'for all'. This is
indeed the art that conceals art!

Sometimes *two* words are thus woven into a pattern of
repetition, a double tautotes, with many of the associated
'fine turns'. In the third stanza of 'Father, Son, and Holy
Ghost' Wesley has already played upon the theme 'all',
and this is continued and even intensified in the following
stanza, with the addition of a twin theme, 'take', introduced
by an epanadiplosis on the preparatory word 'claim' — the
just demand that leads to the only adequate response. The
marriage of the two key words as 'take all' is hinted at or
assumed throughout, though we never see the pair thus
side by side:

> If so poor a worm as I
>   May to thy great glory live,
> All my actions sanctify,

> All my words and thoughts receive:
> Claim me, for thy service claim
> All I have, and all I am.

> Take my soul and body's powers,
>   Take my mem'ry, mind, and will,
> All my goods, and all my hours,
>   All I know, and all I feel,
> All I think, and speak, and do;
> Take my heart — but make it new.[46]

It will be seen that repetition is one of the chief means by which Charles Wesley ensures the powerful impact of the best of his verse. This also is one of the secrets of its continuity and cohesion. It is necessary to examine in a little more detail the architecture both of stanza and of poem, bearing in mind the fact that repetition provides the basic mortar binding together the whole structure and its several components.

8

Structure

Charles Wesley's education had involved another important mental discipline which is less common today, though by no means so rare as the study of rhetoric. He was trained, and to a small extent helped to train others, in the art of logic, though in this field he never pretended to be the equal of his brother John. The very *size* of his stanzas was conditioned by his logical approach. He wanted a stanza in which a theme could be announced, developed, and satisfactorily summarized, preferably with a foreshadowing of the theme for the following stanza. He therefore showed a marked preference for the longer stanza rather than for the somewhat cramping limits of the conventional four lines. On the other hand he carefully avoided as too heavy for lyrical verse the iambic pentameters so beloved of later hymn-writers, and only used lines of more than eight syllables in strongly reflective poems or in his anapaestics, where the length was counteracted by the speed. Such was his fondness for lengthy stanzas that he not only doubled the 8 8.8.8 8.8 metre, but even the already doubled short metre (6.6.8.6) so as to make a stanza of sixteen lines. Yet he mercifully allowed a central pause. This stanzaic caesura is to be found also in most of his eight-lined stanzas — which is why later editors have so easily halved them, though not always without some slight disruption of their thought. Charles Wesley wrote several hundreds of poems in four-lined stanzas, but so appreciated intellectual elbow-room that of his total production of some 27,000 stanzas the over-all average is almost exactly six lines per stanza.

Within the stanzas themselves we find an orderly synchronization of thought and verse. In general every line contains a complete idea, is in fact a clause or sentence, though often this idea spreads over a couplet — rarely is there a break in the middle of a line. Similarly each stanza forms a paragraph, and the whole poem is a logically constructed essay in verse or, to use the contemporary word of his grammar school and university days, a theme. Frequently there is a balancing within the clause or sentence, the line or lines, of both thought and lyrical structure. Corresponding with the verbal device of anaphora is the figure of thought termed parison. This balancing of clauses is the reverse of antithesis, where the thought of one forms a contrast to the thought of the other. Wesley normally combines it with some kind of verbal repetition. One example has already been quoted in the refrain of 'Rejoice, the Lord is king!' — 'Lift up your heart, lift up your voice'.[1] Others will readily come to mind: 'fightings without, and fears within' (from 'And are we yet alive'),[2] and

> Publish at his wondrous birth
> Praise in heaven and peace on earth.[3]

Parison is a favourite device with Wesley for knitting more closely the looser texture of the longer anapaestic line, as in 'Your debt he has paid, and your work he hath done' from 'All ye that pass by',[4] and the following from an unpublished hymn for workers:

> Come let us away,
> And his summons obey
> Who justly demands
> The sweat of our brows, and the work of our hands.[5]

Mr Manning has already drawn attention to Charles Wesley's skilful use of chiasmus. This device, whose name comes from the Greek letter X or 'chi', is the crossing of clauses in the pattern $\begin{smallmatrix} A \\ B \end{smallmatrix} \times \begin{smallmatrix} B \\ A \end{smallmatrix}$. It is almost the equivalent in thought of the verbal figure of antistrophe. the pattern ABBA is often readily distinguishable, as in the For + persons: mercy: : mercy: For + person of:

> For all thy tender mercies are
> If mercy is for me.[6]

Only slightly less obvious are the four nouns of the opening lines of 'The Universal love of Christ':

> Let earth and heaven agree,
> Angels and men be joined ...[7]

As Mr Manning points out, even in that supposedly non-literary poem, 'Jesu, Lover of my soul', there is a very interesting example — nor is this the only one in the hymn:

Just, and holy is Thy name	A
I am all unrighteousness,	B
False, and full of sin I am,	B
Thou art full of truth, and grace.	A

Not only is there the crossed pattern in the four lines as a whole — Saviour: Sinner: :Sinner: Saviour. Mr Manning indicates further examples of chiasmus in these same four lines: one in each of the two pairs AA, BB — personal pronoun: epithet: :epithet: personal pronoun.[8] Actually there are two further examples of a similar type (not noted by Mr Manning) in each of the *consecutive* pairs of lines, AB, BA, in this case epithet: personal pronoun: : personal pronoun: epithet, this time with antithetical instead of parallel ideas.

The question immediately arises, 'Did Wesley think all this out?' The answer must be, I believe, 'No, at least not all of it.' But his mind was so accustomed to manipulating the intertwined formulae of logic as well as the figures of rhetoric that his sentences often quite unconsciously assumed this form of pattern within patterns. Almost always the chiasmus in grammatical arrangement is combined with an antithesis in meaning, as in 'Sow in tears, in joy to reap'[9] and 'Who built the skies, On earth he lies' from the *Nativity Hymns*.[10] The chiasmus is one of the natural outworkings both of the essential paradoxes of the Christian faith and of the antithetical processes of Charles Wesley's literary art.

With this sense of balance in thought as well as in word we are not surprised to note how carefully Charles Wesley articulates his stanzas. As an example we may quote the opening stanza of the 'Hymn of Thanksgiving to the Father' from the *Hymns and Sacred Poems of* 1739 — which incidentally provides a chiasmus in lines 1–2, another in lines 3–4, and a parison in lines 5–6:

> Thee, O my God and King,
> My Father, Thee I sing!
> Hear well-pleased the joyous sound,
> Praise from earth and heav'n receive;
> Lost, I now in Christ am found,
> Dead, by faith in Christ I live.[11]

This stanza is in two distinct sections, as are all the stanzas in this poem, and almost every stanza which Wesley wrote in this particular mixture of iambic and trochaic verse. The opening iambic couplet introduces the theme — in this case a statement of intention — and the succeeding trochaic quatrain develops that theme, in this instance first by expanding the idea of praise introduced in 'sing', and then by showing the reason for that praise, the restoration

of a modern prodigal to his heavenly Father through faith
in Christ. The following stanza similarly announces the
theme of 'father and son' carried over from this one, and
then develops it by an extension of the idea of the wander-
ing of the son and the welcome of the father. And so it
goes on, the careful articulation of each stanza, and of the
stanzas into the poem as a whole.

In this 6 6.8.8.8.8 stanzaic pattern the turning-point in
Wesley's thought is almost always the close of the first
couplet, where the iambics change to trochaics, thought
thus carefully matching metre, or *vice versa*! In other
stanzaic patterns the articulation of Charles Wesley's
thought is quite different, though it is always present —
there is no woolliness in his thinking, no meandering.
Specific stanza-forms were chosen (doubtless almost unconsciously) because they matched specific lines of thought.
Thus Wesley's favourite 8.8.8.8.8 8 iambic metre anounces
and develops the thought during the first four lines and
usually clinches the argument in the closing couplet. Looking for an example at random the first stanza on which my
eye fell was in the trochaic counterpart of the metre which
I sought, 7.7.7.7.7 7:

> Christ, whose glory fills the skies,
>   Christ, the true, the only light,
> Sun of righteousness, arise,
>   Triumph o'er the shades of night:
> Day-spring from on high, be near:
> Day-star, in my heart appear.[12]

Here the theme of Christ the 'light of the world' is introduced by the invocation in lines 1–2 and developed into a
general prayer in lines 3–4; in the parison of the closing
couplet the movement from the general to the particular is
clinched by the direct appeal, 'in *my* heart appear'.

Wherever we look in Charles Wesley's verse we find this

careful development of thought. He does not simply choose his subject and walk round it, describing it from different viewpoints as he comes to them; even less does he drift on by the undisciplined process of the association of ideas; he analyses his theme carefully, and moves in logical succession from one aspect to another. Movement, indeed, is one of the great characteristics of his verse. It is not merely evocative of emotion in a vague way, but takes us step by step along a planned pathway to a definite goal. This is what Mr Manning means when he speaks of the 'liturgical action' of 'Victim Divine', but which he describes perhaps even more felicitously as a 'dramatic and architectural' quality.[13] For it has the virtues of both these realms of art — there is the balanced integration of a carefully designed building, and there is the purposeful movement of a good play. Constantly we are reminded of the technique of drama. We see the plot unfold before our eyes, stanza-scene after stanza-scene to the final dénouement — always an important feature of his verse.

Sometimes this dénouement is unexpected, more often a heightening of emotion at the inevitable climax, sometimes the evocation of a mood of calm resolution to follow the new insight or challenge that has been presented. Like all dramatists, Wesley watched his curtain lines, though one could hardly expect them all to be of equal quality. Mr Manning points out how in 'See how great a flame aspires' every stanza closes with 'a knock-out blow' — 'all the preceding lines lead by steps to an emphatic concluding phrase.'[14] Even more powerful is the closing phrase of stanza 7 of 'Come on, my partners in distress', where Wesley describes the imagined rapture of heaven:

> The Father shining on his throne,
> The glorious co-eternal Son,
> > The Spirit one and seven,

> Conspire our rapture to complete,
> And lo! we fall before his feet,
> And silence heightens heaven.[15]

There is theological and scriptural allusion there in plenty
to keep us busy for some time; in addition, if we've got our
allusions right, and if we've ever been hushed in a soaring
Gothic cathedral, we can hardly miss the awe and the
rightness of the last line.

It is not surprising that Dr Davie quotes Wesley as an
illustration of Ezra Pound's definition of 'scenario' in literary
construction — 'so arranging the circumstance that some
perfectly simple speech, perception, dogmatic statement
appears in abnormal vigour'. Dr Davie draws attention to
'the poignant simplicity which is one of [Wesley's] best
effects ... brought about by sudden and calculated descent
from a relatively elaborate level of language', similar to
King Lear's 'Pray you, undo this button'. As an example he
quotes the following:

> Sinners, believe the gospel word,
>   Jesus is come your souls to save!
> Jesus is come, your common Lord;
>   Pardon ye all through him may have,
> May now be saved, whoever will;
> This man receiveth sinners still.[16]

His comment is: 'The piercing directness of that last line
is an achievement in literary form.'[17] That this is quite
deliberate is confirmed by the fact that in this particular
stanza Wesley deserts his normal articulation for this form,
and instead of pairing his thoughts for a closing couplet
makes the last line stand starkly alone.

Wesley's closing lines are frequently epigrammatic, especially in his satirical verse, but also in his more devotional
poems. In 'Thee, O my God and King', noted above, he

follows the closing words of his prototype, the parable of the Prodigal Son, but makes them evangelical, personal, and epigrammatic, by means of two balanced antitheses:

> Lost, I now in Christ am found,
> Dead, by faith in Christ I live.

A poem on the death of his second child closes on a typical note, though hardly one that we should expect in such a context:

> Love our Eden here would prove,
> Love would make our heaven above.[18]

Love is frequently his closing thought, occasionally in vivid phraseology, such as the closing line of a poem on prayer: 'In speechless eloquence of love'.[19] One of his unpublished poems is a rebuke to those who boast of their Christian perfection, and one feels that the challenging antitheses of the closing epigram are worthy of a better cause:

> Humility your whole delight,
> And your ambition's utmost height
> To weep at Jesus' feet.[20]

Actually Charles Wesley was at his most epigrammatic in his satirical verse, especially upon subjects which moved him greatly, as did the controversy over predestination. 'The Horrible Decree' contains some outstanding examples of vigorous closing lines to the double short metre stanzas:

> And mockest with a fruitless call
> Whom Thou has doomed to die.

> Thou shew'st him heaven, and say'st, Go in —
> And thrusts him into hell.

Indeed the whole of what Charles Wesley calls the 'Other gospel' of the fiend is a sustained epigram, one of the most powerful pieces of theological invective in the English language:

> Sinners, abhor the fiend,
> His *other* Gospel hear:
> 'The God of truth did not intend
>   'The thing his words declare;
>   'He offers grace to all,
>   'Which most cannot embrace,
> 'Mocked with an ineffectual call
>   'And insufficient grace.
>
> 'The righteous God consigned
>   'Them over to their doom,
> 'And sent the Saviour of mankind
>   'To damn them from the womb;
>   'To damn for falling short
>   'Of what they could not do,
> 'For not believing the report
>   'Of that which was not true.
>
> 'The God of love *passed by*
>   'The most of those that fell,
> 'Ordained poor reprobates to die,
>   'And forced them into hell.
>   'He did not do the deed
>   (Some have more mildly raved),
> 'He did not *damn* them — but decreed
>   'They never should be saved.'[21]

Dr Newton Flew has enabled us to see another frequent element in the structure of Charles Wesley's verse, not this time dramatic but homiletic. He was, of course, a preacher, both a logical, a challenging, and a forceful preacher, and it seems obvious (once someone has pointed it out!) that he should prepare many of his poems along the same lines as his sermons. One of the best examples is 'What shall I do my God to love', even though it is a hymn adopted (and slightly adapted) from the closing stanzas of a longer poem. In this closing section he is thinking of Ephesians 3.18–19:, 'To apprehend ... the breadth and length and height and depth, and to know the love of Christ which passeth knowledge.' He announces his text and even outlines his points in the opening stanza:

> What shall I do my God to love,
>   My loving God to praise!
> The length, and breadth, and height to prove,
>   And depth of sovereign grace!

The following stanza is his 'firstly' — the *length* of God's love, which 'to all extends'. Next comes his 'secondly', its *breadth* — 'Throughout the world its breadth is known, Wide as infinity'. Then his 'thirdly', the *height*, both of his own sin, 'grown up to heaven', but also, and even higher still, 'far above the skies', of the soaring mercies of God in Christ. And 'fourthly', 'The *depth* of all-redeeming love', in two stanzas, the second of which (usually omitted from the hymn-books) underlines this idea of depth — 'Deeper than hell ... Deeper than inbred sin'. Having made his points, like any evangelical preacher Charles Wesley 'applies' them in a prayer of supplication. For a final knock-down blow (again omitted from most hymn-books) he works his spatial relationships into a paradox parallel to — though quite different in content from — St Paul's paradox about knowing the love which passes knowledge:

> And *sink* me to perfection's height,
>   The *depth* of humble love.[22]

Sometimes the sermon remains in embryo, as in an instance quoted by Mr Findlay, who points out that the repeated 'Thou' opening three of the lines is for all the world like a preacher announcing his 'heads':

> Saviour in temptation Thou:
>   Thou hast saved me heretofore,
>   Thou from sin dost save me now,
>   Thou shalt save me evermore.[23]

(He might well have added that the opening line announced
the preacher's subject, including the key word, 'Thou'. Nor
should we overlook the concealed artistry of this quatrain:
the two basic words, 'Thou' and 'save' are both introduced
in the opening line, in reverse order, so that there is not
only both the anaphora and the anadiplosis on 'Thou', and
the traductio and mesodiplosis on 'Saviour', 'saved', 'save',
but also a chiasmus between 'Saviour' and 'Thou' in the
opening line and in each of the following three lines.)

Wesley is not unique in achieving this kind of structure,
of course. There are even more notable examples in
Christopher Smart's *A Song to David*. Indeed they are *too*
notable — the machinery tends to creak. The opening
lines of stanza 4 furnish us with a catalogue of David's
virtues:

> Great, valiant, pious, good, and clean,
>   Sublime, contemplative, serene,
>   Strong, constant, pleasant, wise!

The following twelve stanzas each deal (in the same order)
with one of these virtues, and to ensure that the reader
does not miss the point, each epithet opens its respective
stanza, isolated by a dash. Charles Wesley is never as
obvious as that, and is a far greater artist as a result.

We can be left in no doubt that Wesley was adept in the
marshalling of thoughts, as he was of words, and (as we
shall see) of sounds. Yet at the same time he was exceedingly
versatile in varying the methods of his structure in accordance with the material that he was using and the purpose
for which it was intended. He was undoubtedly a master

craftsman in verse. This mastery becomes the more impressive when we consider those deft touches of musical mortar with which he bonded together his structure of thought, whether in stanza or in poem — the 'patterns of sound', to use Mr Findlay's phrase. Wesley's skilful use of repetition for the purpose of emphasis has been sufficiently illustrated, but its use for cohesion has only been hinted at. Many examples could be quoted both of stanzas and of whole poems whose theological theme is accompanied by a musical theme which renders the verse both continuous and compact. One of each must suffice. For a stanza we turn to the following, based on Ephesians 4.4–6:

> Build us in one body up,
> Called in one high calling's hope;
> One the Spirit whom we claim,
> One the pure, baptismal flame,
> One the faith, and common Lord,
> One the Father lives, adored
> Over, through, and in us all,
> God incomprehensible.[24]

The theme is announced in the opening line, and is taken up by the fivefold repetition of 'one' in the five following lines. Wesley is careful, however, not to overdo this repetition, allowing St Paul's 'one Lord' to enter in disguise — 'One the faith, and common Lord' — even though 'One the faith and one the Lord' would have fitted the metre perfectly and would have been nearer to his scriptural original.

This disciplined use of repetition, constantly varied just before it is becoming too obvious, is one of Wesley's strong points, appreciated all the more when turning from Christopher Smart. Stanzas 51–71 of *A Song to David* overdo the word 'ADORATION' (always printed in capitals), and the following stanzas dwell at length on the adjectives 'sweet' (71–4), 'strong', (75–7), 'beauteous' (78–80), 'precious' (81–3), 'glorious' (84–6), and their comparatives. It is all a little too mechanical and obvious, as if he were saying, 'See how clever I am!' Wesley is much more subtle and self-effacing. His delicately modulated repetitions are one of the great secrets of the success of his 'Come, O thou Traveller unknown', underlining its deep emotion, yet never allowing that emotion to become maudlin. (This is the poem, of course, of which Isaac Watts said, 'That single poem, *Wrestling Jacob*, was worth all the verses he himself had written'.)[25] The twin themes of the struggle and the stranger are thus announced in the closing couplets of stanzas 1 and 2:

> With thee all night I mean to stay,
> And wrestle till the break of day.

And:

> But who, I ask thee, who art thou?
> Tell me thy name, and tell me now.

The succeeding three stanzas all end with the same combination of these two themes:

> Wrestling I will not let thee go,
> Till I thy name, thy nature know.

This refrain is omitted from stanza 6, and only partially taken up in the closing couplet of stanza 7:

> I stand, and will not let thee go,
> Till I thy name, thy nature know.

Stanza 8 provides a hesitant answer to half of this recurrent question:

> And tell me, if thy name is Love.

The following stanza triumphantly transforms the question into a proclamation, the order of the elements being also reversed:

> Thy nature, and thy name is Love.

The constant ringing triumph of this same line closes each of the remaining five stanzas, always with a varied introductory line lest the refrain become too mechanical. This is only one element in the poem's literary achievement, but it is a very important one, as it is in many another of Wesley's most successful poems. His poems are integrated artistic structures, not random heaps of building blocks, no matter how decorative.

9

Metre

Another major factor in the literary achievement of
Charles Wesley is his metrical versatility and even — the
word is not too strong — genius. Although he could make
no great musical claims as vocalist, instrumentalist, or
composer, his musical sons acknowledged that his ear was
impeccable. And because there was music in his soul, lilting, rapturous, divine music, he could not be confined to
the humdrum in verse. The lyric was his *métier*. Both his
inventiveness and his mastery in lyrical form were without
parallel in the verse of that century, and perhaps only
paralleled by Shelley in the century that followed. George
Herbert in the previous century exhibited far more
metrical variety than Wesley, but it was the metrical variety
of the philosopher-poet, undoubtedly sincere, yet remarkable for its boundless ingenuity rather than for true lyrical
quality. The Wesleys appreciated Herbert's poetry, but
when John Wesley utilized examples for congregational
singing he found it desirable to restrain their metrical
exuberance by drastic editing. A list of the metres used by
Wesley, with some introductory notes on technical details,
is given in *Representative Verse of Charles Wesley*. (Here, as
there, I use the term 'metre' to cover the varying combina-
tions in length of line, number of lines, syllabic accentuation, and rhyming pattern, which comprises the mechanics
of verse-making, or prosody.)[1] It is sufficient here to make

some general observations about his important place in the story of English prosody, and to illustrate this by some statistics.

The basic nature of English verse has not yet been settled with anything like unanimity, and it seems that in any final formula T.S. Omond's plea for scansion by time-spaces will need to be incorporated with the conventional scansion by syllabic accent. At the very least, however, the conventional description of basically iambic, trochaic, anapaestic, and dactylic feet, with their variants, provides a convenient yard-stick, even though English prosodists may eventually decide to transfer to some as yet unaccepted alternative metrical system, though in fact this still seems far less likely than the transfer of our weights and measures apparatus to the metric system. Let us use what we have while we wait for something better, but realize that it has its drawbacks, and is not foolproof.

By far the greatest bulk of Charles Wesley's verse is in the traditional iambic measure, dignified, safe, though capable of great beauty and power in the hands of an accomplished poet. This is where most versifiers both begin and end. Even the great Isaac Watts rarely ventured outside iambics. His thousand poems include only twenty-two in trochaic metres and five in anapaestics, while his iambics themselves are almost confined to common, long, and short metre. In the best-known collections — the *Psalms* and the *Hymns and Spiritual Songs* — only thirty out of some seven hundred compositions are not in these three basic metres, these thirty being spread over four other metres: 8 8.8.8 8.8; 6 6.8.6 6.8; 6.6.6.6.4.4 4.4; and 10 10.10 10.10 10. Even when we turn to his famous *Horae Lyricae*, so deservedly praised by Dr Samuel Johnson, apart from the thirty-eight pindarics, whose irregular forms place them in a different category, only thirteen examples of eight other metres are to be found. The *Divine Songs* are restricted to the conventional, but the *Moral Songs* add five examples of four anapaestic stanza-forms, and three examples of two trochaic stanza-forms. To summarize, Watts used twenty different stanza-forms, in addition to pindarics and three varieties of couplets. It is fairly clear that he was capable of much more in the way of lyrical experiment, but his position as a pioneer of hymn-writing, at a time when few tunes were available, restricted nine-tenths of his production to the three common iambic forms. With Charles Wesley both the spiritual impulse and the metrical versatility were greater, and the result was a burst of new measures, for some of which the tunes were specially composed, while the remainder were an enrichment of religious verse rather than of congregational worship.

Charles Wesley used no fewer than forty-five iambic metres, and in each of fifteen of them wrote over a thousand lines of verse. The most prolific of all was his favourite form of six eights — 8.8.8.8.8 8, rhyming ABABCC. In this metre he composed over eleven hundred poems, a total of nearly twenty-three thousand lines, most of them with a vigour, a flexibility, yet a disciplined compactness, that proved this to be the instrument fittest for his hand. This, the metre of 'Wrestling Jacob', represents over one-tenth of his total output. His next most prolific form was the old romance metre, 8 8.6.8 8.6, rhyming AABCCB, a metre which moves more rapidly than 8.8.8.8.8 8, but loses in sturdiness what it gains in speed. In this, the metre of Smart's *Song to David*, Charles Wesley wrote over twenty thousand lines in nine hundred poems, including 'O Love Divine, how sweet thou art', and 'Be it my only wisdom here'. The iambic metres next most popular with him were (in order of preference) the cross-rhyming double long metre ('O Thou who camest from above' in its original double form), the double short metre ('Soldiers of Christ arise' and other magnificent marching poems), and the double common metre ('All praise to our redeeming Lord' and 'Sing to the great Jehovah's praise' in their original double form). The production here ranges from just over to just under thirteen thousand lines each. The only rival to these forms was one of the mixed iambic-trochaic metres. Only after these firm favourites with their six or eight lines do we come to the four-lined stanzas: common metre (seven thousand lines), and the cross-rhymed long metre (nine thousand lines). The consecutive-rhyming long metre comes well below nine other metres with twenty-five hundred lines, and the four-lined short metre is among the 'also-rans' with a mere 364 lines.

Putting aside the many experiments which Charles Wesley did not follow up to any great extent, it seems desirable to draw attention to three other iambic metres of which he made considerable use. Only once did he employ the rather flimsy form 6.6.6.6, and very rarely its doubled or consecutively rhyming variations. When strengthened and clinched with a closing octosyllabic couplet, however, it became one of his favourite stanza-forms, used to great effect in 'Let earth and heaven agree', 'Arise, my soul arise', and 'Rejoice, the Lord is king'. Altogether he wrote over three thousand lines in this metre, and a mere 198 in the consecutively rhymed variant, 6 6.6 6.8 8. Wesley wrote almost two thousand lines in the form 7.6.7.6.7.6.7.6, yet never seemed thoroughly happy in it, certainly not as happy as was Cowper in his 'Sometimes a light surprises'. Dr Beckerlegge suggests that Wesley may have been influenced to its use by German example, though he points out that it was also the medium (in continuous form) for Vaughan's 'My soul, there is a country'. In one other even more unusual (and apparently original) stanza-form Wesley did achieve real success. This was the metre of 'Head of thy church triumphant', 7.7.4 4.7 D, in which each half stanza is introduced by one of the unrhyming lines so uncommon in Charles Wesley's verse. In this metre he wrote forty poems amounting to over one thousand lines.

Although the bulk of Charles Wesley's verse was written in iambic measures, however, and although the form 8.8.8.8.8 8 was both his most prolific and his most generally successful, his more original contributions to the development of English prosody were in other types of metre, where his output was not so great in quantity and on the whole not on such a consistently high level of quality. He wrote over one thousand poems (some twenty-two thousand lines) in sixteen trochaic metres, in seven of them writing over one thousand lines each. Again his favourite was an eight-lined stanza — eight sevens, cross-rhymed — in which he wrote over seven thousand lines. The best known example is 'Jesu, Lover of my soul'. One of his more interesting experiments in trochaics is the 8.3 3.6 metre, which he seems to have introduced into English from the German, though John Cennick was also a pioneer in its use — it is the metre of Cennick's 'Ere I sleep, for every favour'.

It is now fairly well known that Charles Wesley played an important part in introducing some anapaestic metres into religious verse, and into hymns in particular, though Professor Elton is hardly accurate in speaking of 'his favourite lolloping anapaestics'. We have seen that Watts wrote five anapaestic poems. Even Prior and Swift, to whom is generally assigned the chief merit for elevating anapaestics from their crudest and clumsiest form in the street ballad to an instrument fit for drawing-room satire, fell very far short of Charles Wesley. Actually their entire combined output of anapaestics does not match in quantity the ninety poems published by Wesley in his most popular anapaestic form. Moreover, his technical mastery is far in advance of theirs, and it is only with Wesley that we really get away from the rather loose elevens and twelves, either in couplets or in stanza-form, to something more taut and shapely. Of the type of stanza formed from two short lines followed by a long one the solitary examples in Prior and Swift (each of whom seems to have written only one) is in the form 5 5.9.5 5.9. Neither has anything to compare with Wesley's regular eight eights, which he wisely and skilfully disciplined to a uniformly iambic opening, thus avoiding the looseness which sometimes characterizes Shenstone's 'Pastoral Ballad' of 1743 — Wesley's possible model. Wesley's popularization of the anapaest in his hymns seems to have been at least as important in improving its status as the somewhat hesitant use made of it by secular poets, and he was a pioneer in making it the medium for the irrepressible lilt of emotions which burst the bonds of conventional verse, as they did of conventional religion. If not responsible for its introduction, it fell to his lot to bring it under firmer discipline and to train it for unaccustomed tasks.

Wesley's experimentation with anapaests began in 1741 with what became easily his most productive form, 5.5.5.5. 6.5.6.5, cross-rhymed, and occasionally set out as 10 10.11 11. It was, of course, an adaptation of the old anapaestic ballad form, with the introduction of what we may call regularized variety, making the stanza both more satisfying aesthetically and more amenable to congregational use. In this form he wrote no fewer than four thousand lines, his hymns including 'O heavenly king' and 'Ye servants of God'. The only other of his eleven anapaestic metres which top the thousand-line mark are the cross-rhyming eight eights mentioned above (exemplified by 'Thou Shepherd of Israel' and the best known of his *funeral* hymns) and the doubled 5 5.5 11 metre of the well known watch-night hymn 'Come, let us anew'. Altogether Wesley wrote some ten thousand lines of anapaestic, or rather iambic-anapaestic verse.

Even more important for the student of prosody is Charles Wesley's fertile experimentation with mixed metres, especially with mixed iambic and trochaic. Once the ear has become accustomed to the syncopated rhythm of these alternations between a rising and a falling beat, there is no gainsaying the force and virility of their challenge. Wesley's first introduction to this alternating beat almost certainly came through the singing of the Moravians, but he made it completely his own, both simplifying it by concentrating on a few basic patterns, and at the same time extending the application of those patterns. His first such experiment was published in 1739, with the form 6 6.7.7.7.7, an opening iambic couplet quickened and strengthened by a cross-rhymed trochaic quatrain. This remained one of his favourite metres, in which he wrote 168 poems, a total of nearly four thousand lines, including 'O Filial Deity'.[2] He next discovered the robust 7.6.7.6.7.7.7.6, cross-rhymed throughout, but with a group of three consecutive trochaic lines opening the second half and breaking the alternating trochaic-iambic sequence. In this he wrote thirty-five hundred lines, including 'God of unexampled grace', and 'Meet and right it is to sing'. He much preferred, however, the variant on which he quickly embarked, in which the alternation both of rhyme and of beat was constant throughout, the fourth trochaic seven being replaced by an iambic eight. This metre was used also by John Cennick from the same year of 1741 in which Wesley published his first example. Altogether Wesley wrote over ten thousand lines in this metre, which thus ranks as his sixth most prolific. Among the 680 poems are 'Lamb of God, whose bleeding love' and 'God of glorious majesty'.[3] None of his other mixed metres occur very frequently, with the exception of one which at first seems like a variant of the romance metre, 8 8.6.8 8.6, the second line being altered from an iambic eight to a trochaic seven. This alteration, however, was undoubtedly an attempt — and a successful attempt — to secure an effect quite distinct from the smoothly running iambics, and Wesley wrote sixty-seven poems (nearly fifteen hundred lines) with this as the basic pattern. Of this, as of the other mixed metres, it is easy to point to a typical example, 'Far from my native land removed', but not to a widely known example, because these unconventional mixtures have not been readily assimilated as hymns, no matter how effective they may be as poems. In mixed metres in general Wesley wrote some twenty thousand lines, about the same as his output in trochaic verse.

Charles Wesley hardly ever ventured into dactylic verse, though (as we shall see) he frequently used an opening choriambus as a variant in his iambic verse, which conveys the dactylic effect of a galloping horse, to whom the iambic reins are speedily applied. He has one famous example of a combination of dactylic and trochaic feet in a hymn written (according to tradition) for use by an open air congregation that was being disturbed by drunken sailors singing 'one of their lewd songs called "Nancy Dawson",' the metre being that of 'Here we go round the mulberry bush', and Wesley's opening line, 'Listed into the cause of sin'.[4]

The eighteenth century was the age of the couplet, and this was almost certainly the vehicle for most of Wesley's lost translations from the classics, as well as much of his reflective and satirical verse. About one hundred such poems are extant, containing over seven thousand lines. Although he experimented in iambic sixes, trochaic sevens, and iambic-anapaestic thirteens, his favourite form of couplets was iambic decasyllables, often with a closing alexandrine. This accounts for fifty poems, a total of over four thousand lines, including his critical *Epistle to the Reverend Mr John Wesley* (1755). Although he also wrote many regular octosyllabic couplets, for much of his political satire he preferred the looser 'Hudibrastics', a mixture of eights and nines, with an occasional longer line. Of these there are thirty examples, comprising about twenty-five hundred lines.

One further minor classification of Wesley's verse may be described as 'varied metres', in the sense that he moves from one to another within the same poem, in order to achieve some particular effect. One interesting example occurs in the *Hymns and Sacred Poems* of 1742, a verse paraphrase of Isaiah 52.7–10. The introductory exclamations — 'How beautiful upon the mountains' etc., verses 7–8, are represented in five stanzas of steady cross-rhyming long metre, but the exhortation 'Break forth into singing' (verse 9) is the signal for him to burst into four stanzas of lilting anapaestics.[5] Even more interesting is a poem discovered at Duke University after *Representative Verse* had reached the page-proof stage. This consists of a series of short lyrics with various stanzaic patterns that form a complex unit with a clear progression in thought, the subject being the death of an unknown Christian. Charles Wesley has no pindaric ode to match those of Isaac Watts, but this document shows that he did in fact experiment with a less elaborate form of ode.[6]

10

Modulations

There is one very important footnote that should be added to any study of Charles Wesley's command of metre. He was for the most part in such perfect command that he never let it dictate to him. In other words he was a poet, rather than a versifier terrified lest an accent might fall 'incorrectly'. Any musician knows that if he remains in the same key for too long monotony sets in. This he avoids by modulations, passages in a different though related key, passages short or long, obvious or subtly concealed beneath the melody, varying both with the occasion and with the technical command and musical sensitivity of the composer. The same kind of thing is true in verse. 'Modulations', as we may call them, are obviously more necessary in longer lines and longer poems, which otherwise would degenerate to a jog-trot. The need is not quite so self-evident in shorter lyrics, but even here their complete absence has a sterilizing effect.

Hymns are in a peculiar category, because they are made for singing to relatively simple tunes, to which each stanza must conform. Hymn writers in general, therefore, tend to ignore (or to remain in ignorance of) the values of modulation. The slavery to the tune is one very important reason for the widespread assumption that hymns cannot be poetry, an assumption based on the (sometimes unrealized) nature of poetry as a constantly varying compromise

between the naturalness of common speech and the artificiality of strictly metrical speech; at the one extreme lies
prose, at the other the hurdy-gurdy. It is broadly true that
hymns with no modulations are as unsatisfactory for reading as those with excessive or violent modulations are for
singing. For the hymn writer with a feeling for poetry the
motto should be 'modulation in moderation'.

Charles Wesley was not simply a hymn writer with a
feeling for poetry, however, but a true poet who wrote
hymns. In his couplets modulation is therefore inevitable,
and the same is true of his 'sacred poems', i.e. the 'hymns'
which were in fact not really intended for regular congregational singing. Even in the true hymns, however, modulation is present. The syncopated beat of the mixed metres
is itself a form of modulation. It is to be found also in
hymns where it is both unexpected and unrealized, being
overlaid by the beat of the music, which is normally remembered even when the verse is being read. If we *do*
conscientiously try to dismiss the tune from our head for
the moment, however, we can hardly fail to realize the
variations in stress and duration of corresponding syllables. One of the most frequent modulations in Wesley's
iambic verse, as in iambic verse generally, is the use of an
opening choriambus, or a foot consisting of a trochee followed by an iambus.[1] This is one of the methods by which
he injects trochaic vigour into the otherwise docile iambics
of the double short metre, witness:

> Soldiers of Christ, arise,
> And put your armour on,
> Strong in the strength which God supplies
> Through his eternal Son;
> Strong in the Lord of hosts,
> And in his mighty power,
> Who in the strength of Jesus trusts
> Is more than conqueror.[2]

This is by no means 'regular' verse, as many unsuspecting folk assume. Out of the eight lines four begin with the deliberately misplaced beat of a choriambus — the first, third, fifth, and seventh. This looks at first almost like a regular pattern of misplaced beats, but no! In the second stanza it is the first and seventh lines only, in the third stanza the first, third, and seventh, while the fourth line opens with what is more like a spondee. In the fourth stanza only the first line begins with a choriambus, and in the fifth there are two pyrrhic feet, consisting of relatively unstressed syllables. Usually these accentual variations are not sufficiently marked to cause a worshipper discomfort. In this particular instance the *Methodist Hymn-Book* (1933, 484) set the hymn to *From Strength to Strength*, a tune specially written for the syncopated beat of the first stanza, so that it misfires (though only slightly) in other stanzas. This strong tune was also brought over into *Hymns and Psalms* (719), to which was added as an alternative a traditional four-line tune in regular iambic measure, *St Ethelwald*; in the 1933 volume this had been set to No. 581, Doddridge's 'Ye servants of the Lord', which also contains some syncopation, but less marked. 'Soldiers of Christ', of course, was in fact originally written as a lengthy poem, in the course of which Wesley felt it necessary, as well as permissible, to vary his scheme of accentuation.

The opening choriambus is by no means confined to this metre, as may be seen from the first lines of two well-known hymns linked with Charles Wesley's conversion: 'Where shall my wond'ring soul begin', and 'O for a thousand tongues to sing'. 'And can it be that I should gain' (also suggested as the hymn written immediately following Wesley's conversion) has also been treated as if it opened with a choriambus, although it is much more regular, with fewer examples of the choriambus. The *Methodist Hymn-Book* (371) tried to squeeze it into the robust tune *Sagina*, with some awkward results. The tune was very popular, however, and so was retained in *Hymns and Psalms*, which introduced *Didsbury* as an alternative; this caters for a choriambus in the first four lines with an iamb in each of the closing two lines, again not completely satisfactory. With such a deliberately flexible poet as Charles Wesley it is almost impossible to design a tune which would perfectly fit every line of every verse of one of his hymns. The opening choriambus is often combined with less noticeable variations, as in the line, 'Pardon, and holiness, and heaven' which occurs in two of his well-known hymns, 'Thou hidden source of calm repose' (*Collection* 201:12, *Hymns and Psalms*, 275:12), and 'Author of faith, eternal Word' (*Collection* 92:16, *Hymns and Psalms*, 662:16) Here, in addition to the opening choriambus, there is a distinct lightening of the emphasis on '-ness', where the beat would regularly fall, though there is a compensatory lengthening of this syllable through the presence of a closing sibilant.

This brief discussion of only one form of modulation — though probably the most important — enables us to see that there is more of the mystery of music in many of Charles Wesley's hymns than is at first obvious, especially when the ear is deafened by a familiar tune. That Wesley's use of modulation is significant in the general history of prosody may be seen by quoting some words from Mr Sampson's *Concise Cambridge History of English Literature:* 'To us the substitution of a three-syllabled foot for a two-syllabled foot and the replacing of an "iamb" with its "rise" by a "trochee" with its "fall" are neither faults nor anomalies, but the touches that transmute metre into rhythm. In listening to Chatterton and Blake and Coleridge we must not take these things for granted; we must make an imaginative retreat in audition, and hear the liberties of the new poetry as they first fell upon ears attuned to the regularity and smoothness practised by the poets who came after Pope, and prescribed by the theorists who formulated the principles they expected the poets to practice. But the end of the century saw many signs of revolt against mechanical regularity.'[3] In fact the signs had been there long before the poets named; indeed in the variety and freedom of his rhythm as well as in the rapturous content of his verse Charles Wesley may be regarded as one of the heralds of the Romantic Revival. It is somewhat strange that in spite of his recognition of Charles Wesley's literary stature Mr Sampson seems to have missed the fact that in this matter of 'substitution' (as he prefers to call it) Wesley was in the vanguard of the reformers.[4]

As a pendant I should perhaps add that not all the modulations which today we find in Wesley's verse are intentional. Many result from a shift in accent since his day. One example may be given. In 'Come, sinners, to the Gospel feast'[5] Charles Wesley wrote the following balanced iambic couplet, each line opening with a choriambus:

> This is the time, no more delay
> This is the acceptable day.

The lines are perfectly all right so long as we stress the first syllable of 'acceptable', as did eighteenth century Englishmen. With the modern shifting of the accent to the second syllable, however, the effect is to have one stressed followed by three unstressed syllables, and the line is thrown out of joint. In actual fact Methodists did try to sing this until 1933, when the line was amended to 'This is the Lord's accepted day'. Not every such example was amended, however. In No. 156 of the 1933 hymn-book a similar line is left unchanged, so that it reads like an anapaestic rather than an iambic line:

> Make this the acceptable hour;
> Come, O my soul's physician Thou!

Hymns and Psalms (150:21) alter this to read: 'Make this my Lord's accepted hour'. The chief sinners in this matter of shifted accent are listed by Dr Bett as 'ac'ceptable', 'ce'mented', 'con'fessor', 'obdu'rate', and 'suc'cessor'.[6]

11

Rhymes

Most of us find it far easier to detect the music of the rhyme than the more subtle music of the rhythm with its variations in stress and tempo. Charles Wesley recognized rhythm as a far more important element in poetry than rhyme, even though he seems never to have experimented in blank verse, and never took the easy way followed by Watts and others of being content with two rhyming lines per quatrain. It is, I believe, his matured sense of the respective importance of these elements of rhythm and rhyme, rather than his subordination of poetry to piety (as suggested by G. H. Vallins) that leads to the frequent imperfection of his rhymes. If rhyme had impressed him as supremely important he would have thrown overboard many otherwise worthy lines, or at least remodelled them. He knew, however, that rhyme was a useful auxiliary rather than of the essence of poetry, and so (as Vallins succinctly remarks) 'he used it as a servant, but did not submit to it as a master'.[1]

Some Charles Wesley enthusiasts have proclaimed him as a master of rhyme in a quite different sense: they can find no spot or blemish in this aspect of his verse. Alas! this is surely blind (or deaf) worship! I admit, of course, that several cautions must be entered before criticizing the rhymes of Wesley's day — or, for that matter, of any day but our own. Many rhymes perfectly acceptable to an

eighteenth century ear sound clumsy now because of
changing usages in ordinary speech. Sometimes these
changes are mere nuances of pronunciation, but occasionally they are much more obtrusive, involving not only the
transformation of vowel sounds but also (as we have seen)
the shift of the accent from one syllabe to another. Dr Bett
carefully analyses both aspects of this subject, and points
out the following as perfectly good rhymes for the meticu-
lous Pope and his contemporaries: 'join/mine' and 'oil/smile',
'shower/pour', 'wound/found', 'convert/heart', 'great/feet',
'God/rod' *and* 'God/road'.[2]

Another possible source of unjustified criticism is the
failure to recognize the poets' agreement that an 'eye-
rhyme' like 'come/home' might occasionally serve as an
understudy for an 'ear-rhyme'. Obviously this is a conven-
tion which must not be abused, for poetry is after all an
appeal to the ear, even when it approaches the ear silently
by way of the eye and the mind.

There is yet another point of criticism to be considered
in this matter of Wesley's rhymes. A number of them are
perfect to the ear, but not to the mind, because they break
accepted grammatical conventions. As an example we turn
to the second stanza of 'Jesu, united by thy grace', which
would doubtless be much more popular but for one jarring
word:

> Still let us own our common Lord,
>   And bear thine easy yoke,
> A band of love, a threefold cord,
>   Which never can be broke.[3]

This sounds either careless or criminal to the literary
purist of today, yet caused no offence in Wesley's own
time. His contemporaries knew that 'broke' had not merely
hobbled in to patch up the rhyme — it was a valid alternative for 'broken'. Within, as well as at the end of his lines,

Charles Wesley continually uses unfamiliar grammatical forms, or, more frequently, familiar forms in unfamiliar settings. He chooses each particular form for a particular reason, whether it be rhythm, rhyme, or music, but we can be sure that in almost every case no one in his own day would adjudge him guilty of a solecism. It is always wise when meeting any peculiar grammatical usage in the writings of either of the Wesley brothers (or of other scholarly writers in that and previous ages) to assume that it is an example of differing customs rather than of differing standards. The Wesleys lived in a period of grammatical flux, and in his verse Charles Wesley sometimes made the best of both worlds. The fluidity was most noticeable in the past participle, which was frequently assimilated to the past tense — Gray's famous *Elegy* was originally described as 'wrote in a country church-yard'.[4]

When all the excuses have been made, however, Charles Wesley must plead guilty to having written, writ, or wrote many imperfect rhymes. Without labouring the point, we may instance the opening stanza of a well-known hymn where *every* rhyme is faulty, though one is an 'eye-rhyme':

> Behold the servant of the Lord!
> I wait thy guiding hand[5] to feel,
> To hear, and keep thine every word,
> To prove, and do thy perfect will.
> Joyful from all my works to cease,
> Glad to fulfil all righteousness.

Wesley, like most other writers of English verse, found it difficult to secure enough varied and pleasing feminine rhymes — the double rhymes consisting of an accented followed by an unaccented syllable. In any case he much preferred the masculine ending, quite apart from the fact that because the accent was on the closing syllable it was necessary to seek a rhyme for that syllable alone. Indeed

because of this strong preference it is usually possible to
say from a glance at the syllabic structure of his stanzas
whether they are iambic, trochaic, or mixed: six or eight
syllables normally mean three or four iambic feet, ending
with an accented syllable; seven usually mean three trochaic
feet, again ending with an accented monosyllable; and a
combination of six and/or eight with seven normally
implies a combination of iambic and trochaic, in each case
with closing accents for each line. This is by no means
invariable, of course, with a poet of his versatility, but it is
true in well over ninety per cent of his verse.

Nevertheless Wesley was at least moderately successful
with the feminine rhyme, especially in the lighter form of
Hudibrastic verse, where such rhymes as 'walk in/talking'
and 'wearing/appear in' do not seem so incongruous as
they might do in hymns, even hymns in the lighthearted
anapaestic measure. As a matter of fact both examples
quoted *do* appear in a hymn, and a well-known one — 'O
what shall I do my Saviour to praise', from *Hymns and
Sacred Poems* of 1742.[6] They are there printed as *internal*
rhymes, however, where mere assonance might suffice. If
we turn to the trochaic forms which forced him to frequent
feminine rhymes we see Wesley beset with the same kind
of difficulty, and often apparently not really worried
whether he overcomes it smoothly or not. His best known
hymn in that metre is probably 'Love Divine, all loves
excelling'.[7] In that poem he uses the following imperfect
feminine rhymes: 'compassion/salvation', 'deliver/never',
'blessing/ceasing', 'glory/before Thee'. I do not add 'Spirit/
inherit' because this *was* an acceptable rhyme, the
contemporary pronunciation of 'spirit' approximating to
'sperit'. Occasionally his feminine rhymes consist of
diphthongs such as 'fires/desires', which is tolerable, and
'cares/snares', which to a modern ear certainly sounds like
a masculine rhyme.

It is noteworthy that the rare stanza-forms in which Wesley used an unrhyming line were so framed in order to avoid the necessity of an added feminine rhyme, namely the iambic 7.7.4 4.7 D, and the related iambic-anapaestic variant 7.7.5 5.8; the unrhyming line in the trochaic example, 8.7.8.7.4.7, also has a feminine ending. Only in the first form noted did Wesley write any considerable number of poems — forty, a total of over one thousand lines. It led him to some strange expedients, as may be seen by looking at his most well-known hymn in that metre, 'Head of thy church triumphant': 'adore Thee/glory', 'fire/ nigher', 'favour/ever', 'Stephen/heaven'.[8] It also led to the ingenuity of the 'verb plus preposition' rhyme in one of his *Hymns for Times of Trouble* (1744):

> Some put their trust in chariots,
> And horses some rely on,
>> But God alone
>> Our help we own,
> God is the strength of Sion.[9]

We may sum up Wesley's attitude to feminine rhymes by saying that he did not really enjoy himself when he was writing under this type of discipline, and much preferred the strong masculine ending. Altogether he wrote a mere three hundred poems in metres which called for them, out of a total of some nine thousand.

A few sentences at least should be added about the more subtle forms of verbal music. To Wesley's sensitive ear individual words had a melodic as well as a factual content, and occasionally their musical outweighed their intellectual value. We never find him deserting sense for sound, but he frequently rejected a word of simple sense and simple music for another which was harder to understand but contained more subtle or more rousing music. This is true of his classical vocabulary, examples being the beauty of 'amaranthine' and the sinewy strength of polysyllables like 'inextinguishable' and 'incomprehensible'. It is true also of his use of many biblical names such as Jeshurun and Zerubbabel. This also was an important factor in his manuscript revisions. Even his images were as likely to appeal to the ear as to the eye, for as a handmaid of religion music attracted him far more than did art.[10]

12

Poems or Hymns?

It can be proved conclusively that Charles Wesley wrote far more than 'between six and seven thousand hymns', even after subtracting John Wesley's known contribution and after defining a hymn as 'a lyrical poem with mainly religious content', thus disqualifying the few hundreds of his nine thousand poems which are not even faintly religious. On the other hand it can also be demonstrated that the use of a still narrower definition will reduce Charles Wesley's quota of hymns to the more modest proportions of some three or four thousand — the actual figure will depend in part on the assessment of many borderline cases, and must therefore be left somewhat vague. Nor is this simply a matter of statistics, so that what is lost on the roundabouts of one definition is gained on the swings of another. Not only Charles Wesley but the literate public at large has suffered from the conventional attitude that Charles Wesley was a hymn writer who occasionally stumbled into the realms of poetry in those hymns. Professor H. N. Fairchild, for instance, in the second volume of his *Religious Trends in English Poetry* (1942), confesses that 'the hymns of Charles Wesley ... may so often be regarded as personal religious lyrics, and good ones, that here I have been tempted to abandon my policy of excluding hymnody from the scope of these studies'. He adds in a footnote that his scheme does not prevent him from glancing 'at the hymns of poets like Cowper, who also wrote non-liturgical religious poetry'. Yet in actual fact Charles Wesley wrote much more 'non-liturgical religious poetry' than did Cowper, and Professor Fairchild might therefore with an easy conscience have followed his intuition. Far from being a writer of hymns only, albeit very good ones, we believe that Charles Wesley was primarily a devotional poet, though he deliberately diverted much of his output for congregational use, and other poems were so diverted for him. He wrote, however, because he *had* to, not mainly because he wanted to supply singable spiritual ditties for the people called Methodists. Both his hymns and his poetry are better understood and appreciated if this is borne in mind.

Some attempt at defining a hymn is obviously necessary if we are to assess Charles Wesley's position in the history of religious verse. How should a hymn be defined? (Perhaps we should ask instead, 'How *can* a hymn be defined?' for even Julian's *Dictionary of Hymnology* makes no attempt to tell us what hymns really are!) The *Shorter Oxford English Dictionary* offers the following definition: 'song of praise to God; spec[ifically] a metrical composition adapted to be sung in a religious service'. The first part of this definition (based on that of St Augustine) is both too general and too restricted, for it overlooks the frequent elements of confession or prayer in hymns. The specific definition brings us much nearer to what most of us understand by the term, though it seems nevertheless desirable to essay a closer analysis of the elements of such a composition. The normal English hymn can be distinguished from related species of verse, I suggest, by reference to four criteria, two concerned with its content and two with its form:

1. It is *religious*, an act of worship.
2. It is *communal* in its approach to religion, containing sentiments which may be shared by a group of people, even though they may all be expected to sing 'I' instead of 'we'.

3. It is *lyrical*, written to be sung, not chanted or intoned.

4. It is comparatively *regular* both in metre and in structure, and consists of at least two stanzas.

All these criteria may admit of slight variation, but they form the basic ingredients of what we usually recognize as a hymn, a species which includes the variety known as the 'metrical psalm'. If all four elements are not present to a marked degree, then it would be better to speak of the composition by some specific name appropriate to its special function, such as anthem, chant, chorus, doxology, or else (to use Charles Wesley's own term) as a 'sacred poem'.

No such definition can be so absolutely satisfactory as to erect a watertight barrier between hymns and poems, and there will still be room for disagreement in its application to particular examples. In practice, also, many of Charles Wesley's compositions slip without warning from one category to another. In spite of overlapping and uncertainty, however, the religious verse of Charles Wesley undoubtedly falls into two main categories. It seems clear also that Charles Wesley himself fully recognized this fact. The first two volumes of religious verse edited and published by John Wesley (in 1737 and 1738) were both entitled *A Collection of Psalms and Hymns*. When Charles Wesley began to share the responsibility for publication in the following year his name appeared on an altered title-page — *Hymns and Sacred Poems*. Three volumes with this title and over the names of the two brothers appeared in rapid succession, in 1739, 1740, and 1742, and a further anonymous one — mainly a selection from the 1739 volume for use in Ireland — in 1747. To make the responsibility for this title clearer, Charles Wesley used it for the two-volume work which was published in his name alone in 1749. John Wesley's own predilection seems to have been for 'Collection' — one might say that he was the born editor as Charles was the born creator. John issued another *Collection of Psalms and Hymns* in 1741, and this title was retained even after the second edition of 1743 saw the addition of Charles Wesley's name to the title-page and the filling out of the work with his poems. Nor did John forsake the word in issuing his three-volume anthology in 1744 — it was still a 'Collection' of 'Moral and Sacred Poems'. The same key word designated his most famous 1780 hymn-book — *A Collection of Hymns for the use of the People called Methodists.*

The religious lyrics in which Charles Wesley excelled were described by him, therefore, as 'Hymns and Sacred Poems', the two terms flowing into each other rather than forming mutually exclusive categories. Their varied character may be illustrated from the contents of the 1749 volumes. Perhaps half are hymns in the specific sense as defined above; a few are paraphrases of scripture; and a great many are poems written on particular occasions, such as 'After a deliverance from death by the fall of an house', or 'Written in going to Wakefield to answer a charge of treason'. While recognizing and proclaiming that his compositions were by no means all hymns, however, Charles Wesley does tend to use the term 'hymn' in a generic rather than in a specific sense. Of the 455 pieces in the two volumes, 392 are explicitly described by that term. In actual fact most critics would probably agree that many of these are really 'sacred poems', even though parts of them at least might have been used on rare occasions as hymns. For Charles Wesley himself, as for others, there were many compositions at each end of the scale which were quite distinct from each other, and must be classed either as hymns or as sacred poems. In the middle, how-ever, were many which could be described as both or either, and the choice of term would depend on the use made of the composition — a sacred poem could be sung as a hymn, and a hymn could be used in private like a

devotional poem. Because of this extensive overlapping
Charles Wesley eventually came to use the shorter and
simpler term 'hymn' as a generic term embracing the
'sacred poem'. Both instalments of *Hymns on God's Everlasting Love* (1741) contain items which cannot possibly be
described as hymns in any specific sense; perhaps Wesley
considered *Hymns and Sacred Poems on God's Everlasting Love*
as a possible title, but if so he rejected it in the interests of
brevity. Similarly, although the first *Funeral Hymns* (1746)
did in fact consist exclusively of hymns (many of them with
a strongly individual connotation), the second series (1759)
contains many which are really elegies, though it seems just
possible that they may have been used on a single occasion
in public worship. In his *Short Hymns on Select Passages of the
Holy Scriptures* Charles Wesley finally gave up any idea of
discriminating between the two categories. The bulk of the
collection consists of poems which are either irregular in
form, complicated in metre, or far from communal in
theme, and in fact very few were ever used as hymns.
The term 'sacred poem', however, had been dropped,
apparently for good, and the literary world henceforth
thought of Charles Wesley as a 'mere' writer of hymns. For
this erroneous conclusion he himself must clearly carry a
share of the responsibility.

13

The Study of the Wesleys' Hymns

Between 1739 and 1745 John and Charles Wesley published five major volumes as joint authors, with no indi-
cation of the extent of their respective contributions.
These five volumes, together with John Wesley's *Collection
of Moral and Sacred Poems* of 1744, which again contained
compositions of undifferentiated Wesley authorship, together with a hymn-pamplet of 1746, between them offer
over seven hundred poems which are either original or
are adaptations from earlier poets. These adaptations
in the earlier publications include over forty from George
Herbert, most heavily edited, over thirty translations
from German hymns, and transcriptions and abridgments
from many other writers, some of them (especially in
the 1741 volume) still unidentified, a total of over two
hundred which are not strictly original. This leaves some
five hundred poems which are probably the original compositions of one or other of the brothers. These five
hundred pieces, however, include many of the classical
Wesley hymns and poems. After 1746 it seems that John
Wesley wrote hardly any original verse, with the notable
exception of his lament for the loss of Grace Murray
in 1749. He confined himself to praising or criticizing
particular examples of his brother's lavish output, and

editing them for the successive general hymn-books of Methodism.

In agreeing not to distinguish their respective contributions to the joint publications the brothers did nothing to ease the lot of inquisitive students anxious to bestow credit where it truly belongs. The careful study of Methodist hymnology, however, was of late and slow growth.

It is to Samuel Bradburn that we owe the statement: 'He [John] told me that he and his brother agreed not to distinguish their hymns from each other's.'[1] Bradburn's frequent and close contacts with John Wesley gave him ample opportunity to discuss such matters: 'I have slept with him hundreds of nights; I have travelled with him thousands of miles. I lived in what he reckoned, more immediately, his own family, in London, and Bristol, five years together: I knew his opinions, his disposition, and the very secrets of his heart.'[2]

There can be no question, of course, that the great bulk of the Wesley verse, both in those volumes with acknowledged joint authorship, in the 1780 *Collection*, and in their *Poetical Works* as a whole, came from the pen of Charles. John Wesley said as much in his Preface to the *Collection*: 'But a small part of these hymns are of my own composing.'[3] Most of their friends and followers seem simply to have taken for granted their rich heritage of Christian song, without asking questions. A few, however, remained curious, and sought fuller details about the specific bequests from each brother. Clearly Bradburn had been one who questioned John about the matter. John's first biographer, John Hampson, added little to the evidence of the 1780 preface: 'Among [their publications] are the hymns on different occasions, written chiefly by Mr Charles Wesley, which are very numerous, and which we dismiss with observing that the *Funeral* and *Scripture Hymns* are in general the best.'[4]

Robert Southey, the Poet Laureate, in his *Life* of John, did not address the problem of the brothers' joint responsibility, but did pay notable tribute to the high quality of the Methodist hymns in general. Of John's 1780 *Collection* he said: 'Some few ... were selected from various authors; some were his own composition; but far the greater part were by his brother Charles. Perhaps no poems have ever been so devoutly committed to memory as these, nor quoted so often upon a death-bed ...[The Methodists] sing with the spirit and the understanding also ...in psalms and hymns which are both sense and poetry, such as would sooner provoke a critic to turn Christian than a Christian to turn critic.'[5]

Richard Watson, who in his 1820 *Observations* had defended Methodism against some of Southey's less perceptive remarks, in 1831 wrote his own more sympathetic biography of Wesley, and in a very lengthy footnote tried to recover the high status of the early Wesley hymns from the mistaken ascriptions of James Montgomery's *Christian Psalmist* (1825), showing that the brothers had published them long before the Moravian *Collection* of 1754. He wrote: 'How many of the ... translations were from the pen of John, and how many were by Charles, will never now probably be ascertained ... Some have, indeed, attributed the whole of the translations from the German to John, as supposing that Charles did not well understand German. But of this we have no decisive evidence ... Certainly there is internal evidence ... of Charles's manner. John's versions are generally more polished and elegant; Charles had more fire, and was more careless.'[6] In 1841 Watson's London colleague, Thomas Jackson, published profuse and valuable details about the background of dozens of Charles's own hymn publications, but said little about John's specific contributions, except a casual reference under 1740 to 'several admirable translations from the German, which doubtless came from the pen of John'.[7]

Not until 1848 was there a serious and comprehensive study of Methodist hymnology, and that was by an American, David Creamer. Creamer mentioned Bradburn's testimony, and recounted the efforts of Richard Watson and Thomas Jackson to discover the history of the Wesleys' publications, including the differentiation of the early verse of one brother from that of the other. Creamer espoused Jackson's view that at least the German hymns had been translated by John, not Charles, as Watson had thought, and suggested that by identifying all the hymns of Charles, the residue could then be assigned to John.[8]

In 1868 Dr George Osborn began his five-year task of collecting the Wesleys' poems. He announced that although most of the Wesley hymn publications were anonymous, yet 'all [were] capable of being certainly identified'.[9] With Vol.V he completed Charles Wesley's *Hymns and Sacred Poems* of 1749, commenting on Charles's complete responsibility for them, and especially on John's disavowal of 'those passages which favour the notion that to those who are perfected in love, apostasy is impossible.'[10] With the conclusion of Vol.VIII he had dealt with all the jointly published verse, and was about to turn to Charles Wesley's hymns on scripture, both in print and in manuscript. To those who had requested the half-promised identification of the poems by John he stated that he had decided to respect the apparent desire of both brothers for anonymity, 'especially as any distinction now attempted must be to a great extent, if not wholly, conjectural.' He went on, however, to venture his own conjecture on the subject: 'He hopes to be excused for observing that his own inquiries have led him to think it likely that Mr John Wesley contributed more largely to these joint publications than is commonly supposed; and that the habit of attributing almost everything found in them to his brother is scarcely consistent with a due regard to accuracy.'[11] In the preface to Vol.IX Osborn felt compelled to note some of Charles's weaknesses: 'His interpretations of unfulfilled prophecies ... His early tendencies toward the system of the mystics ...; an apparent want of harmony between' John and Charles with regard to Christian perfection. He also pointed out that because of this disharmony he had inserted in the *Poetical Works* John's critical marginal comments in his own copy of his brother's *Short Hymns.*[12]

With the Wesleys the problem of authorship is inextricably linked with that of publication. In only a relatively small proportion of instances do we have absolute proof in either field, only circumstantial evidence with varying degrees of probability. Even the evidence of handwriting is not always conclusive, because each brother occasionally made copies of the other's compositions, or acted as his publishing agent.[13] Even when John added poems by Charles to his prose publications he rarely named Charles as author, which may occasionally have irked the younger brother, in spite of the agreed anonymity of their verse publications.

This whole question of anonymity is puzzling, and more extensive than is usually realized. Altogether the two brothers issued eighty verse publications of various kinds between 1727 and 1788, not counting component parts and reissues. Of these four bore the name of John on the title-page, eight that of Charles, and six their joint names, the remaining sixty-two being completely anonymous. Of these anonymous publications strong circumstantial evidence indicates that the responsibility for publishing in ten instances was that of John, in forty-seven that of Charles; sometimes the case needs building up carefully, and in five instances remains open. Even if the responsibility for *publishing* is fairly clear, there still remains the question of the *authorship* of the individual components, which again can in most instances be decided only by circumstantial evidence, though the fact of publication may often prove one important element in that evidence. This small volume is hardly the forum for debating the force of the varied clues, which will be presented in the forthcoming bibliography of the brothers' publications.

The early agreement made between John and Charles about this anonymous publishing (clearly applying only if neither of them was solely responsible for the material) was probably quite simple in its origin, but may well have developed complexities when Charles began to challenge the ascendancy of John, his elder by five years. The perhaps subconscious sibling rivalry developed into a crisis in 1749, when Charles broke up John's unconsummated marriage to Grace Murray; it reached another crisis over their differing views of Christian perfection around 1760; and the worst crisis of all in 1784, because of John's readiness to support the clerical ambitions of his lay preachers, even by ordination. Charles's manuscript poems reflect much of this rivalry, but for the most part it was not aired through their publications, and was partly obscured by this very device of anonymity. Charles increasingly retreated into the Methodist background, though he retained a few staunch advocates of his own viewpoints.

The two brothers did indeed differ radically on many minor points, and on some major points, especially in their teaching on Christian perfection. This proved a major factor in Charles Wesley's publication of his *Short Hymns on Select Passages of the Holy Scriptures* (two volumes, 1762), as Dr Osborn pointed out, and was reflected in John's marginal comments. One of the most peculiar episodes in this semi-estrangement had taken place in the previous year, however. Two general Methodist hymn-books were

published in 1761, with some minor overlapping of content. The best known was published by John, *Select Hymns
with Tunes Annext*, the other by Charles, *Hymns for those to
whom Christ is all in all*. I had hoped that this latter work
might offer strong evidence about Charles's own original
contributions to the early volumes of hymns. Unfortunately
this was not the case. In preparing it he went solidly
through eight sources in roughly chronological order: the
three joint volumes of *Hymns and Sacred Poems*, his own
Hymns for ...Redemption and the 1749 *Hymns and Sacred
Poems*; then he turned to the joint *Hymns on the Lord's
Supper* and the undifferentiated Wesley items in Vol.3 of
his brother's *Moral and Sacred Poems*. Alas, it is quite clear
that in this exercise Charles did not restrict himself to
his own poems. Probably because he was using joint publications, he seems to have felt no qualms about selecting
some of those clearly prepared by his elder brother from
Herbert and the Germans. Other interesting points do
arise, however. My major new discovery was that this
volume, apparently ignored at first by John, eventually
became the source of some centos of their early poems
which John later incorporated in his 1780 *Collection*.[14]

It seems fairly certain that Charles published this volume
as an antidote to John's acquiescence in the claims to
Christian perfection made by some of the Methodists, their
revival-stirred emotions apparently clouding their critical
judgment, and leaving them susceptible to moral weak-
ness. On the other hand, Charles was also protesting
against John's watering down of 'sinless perfection' to
situation ethics, and against John's increasing doubt that
perfection might be 'given instantaneously, in a moment'.
As a corrective against such matters he noted in his prefixed 'Advertisement' that 'those to whom Jesus Christ "is
made of God wisdom and righteousness and sanctification"'
need 'not only the witness but the fruit of his Spirit ...

They labour to "abstain from all appearance of evil", and are "zealous of good works".' This furnishes a reminder that whenever any hint of antinomianism crept into a hymn — though to this John also objected strongly — it was even less likely to be introduced by Charles than by John.[15] John thought that Charles 'set perfection too high', yet recognized the merit in Charles's approach, and insisted: 'Go on, in your own way, [in] what God has peculiarly called you to. Press the *instantaneous* blessing; then I shall have more time for my peculiar calling, enforcing the *gradual* work.'[16]

There was probably a subtle challenge to his brother in the very title chosen by Charles for his 1761 book. Both brothers remembered that it was John who in 1741 had first published Charles's 24-stanza 'The Promise of Sanctification' as an appendix to his own sermon, *Christian Perfection*[17], and that they had jointly reprinted it in their 1742 *Hymns and Sacred Poems*. And from its closing line he had drawn the title for this 1761 volume: 'Purge me from every sinful blot ... Give me a new, a perfect heart ... In every point thy law obey, And perfectly perform thy will ... From actual, and from inbred sin, My ransomed soul persist to save ... Now let me gain perfection's height! Now let me into nothing fall! Be less than nothing in thy sight, and feel that Christ is all in all.'

14

The Major Problem: John or Charles?

We may now begin to apply our general observations to the specific problem that has plagued Methodist hymnologists for over a century: for which individual hymns within the joint publications of the two Wesley brothers was John responsible, for which Charles?

By way of preamble, however, perhaps another question should be asked, which to my knowledge has never been considered. Is it possible that the brothers not only engaged in the joint publication of volumes but in the joint creation of individual hymns? There are plenty of examples of each brother's repeating his own lines, John as a rhetorical device of repetition within a hymn, both John and Charles as a retrieval from memory of a line in another poem. But what are we to think about one brother repeating a rhymed pair of lines from what appears to be the verse of the other? Is this an instance of copying, of employing a phrase from the subconscious mind, or of suggesting a change while reading or hearing the other's manuscript? Should this be regarded as strong evidence that both passages actually originated with the same writer?

The *Hymns and Sacred Poems* of 1739 furnish an interesting example. 'Jesu, whose glory's streaming rays' was (in accordance with a generally sound tradition) translated from the German of W. Deszler by John Wesley; 'And can it be that I should gain' was traditionally written by Charles. 'Jesu ...' is found in the last hymn in Part I, p. 100, 'And can ...' on pp. 118–19. Both contain the rhyming lines: 'No condemnation now I dread /.../ Alive in thee, my living head /...' Each pair occurs in a cross-rhymed quatrain, the first at the close of the fourth stanza, the second at the beginning of the sixth stanza; nor is the context of either verbally related to the context of the other. The arrangement of the hymns is so haphazard that we cannot claim that the first printed is necessarily earlier than the second. The translation of the first is so free that the words do not arise automaticaly from the German, though they do represent its meaning. To treat this duplication as pure coincidence is surely less logical than to affirm that the identical phrases are probably the work of a single author, if not himself *writing* both passages, at least strongly influencing the other in some way.

There are dozens of examples of duplicate lines and phrases in the 1780 *Collection* alone which may well offer some evidential value about their authorship, though perhaps never conclusive proof. Normally the presumption would be, however, that the duplicated lines were written by the same brother, whose identity would need to be decided (if possible) on other grounds.[1]

Some of these duplications undoubtedly raise necessary questions, but occasionally they may supply answers. Three co-ordinated duplications in one poem is beyond coincidence. One lengthy hymn in *Hymns and Sacred Poems* of 1742 has long been under dispute. It is entitled 'The Lord's Prayer Paraphrased', and begins, 'Father of all, whose powerful voice'. John Wesley appended this poem to his sixth discourse upon the Sermon on the Mount, with the introductory words, 'I believe it will not be unacceptable to the serious reader to subjoin' — which might well have been followed by 'a hymn by my brother', though no composer was named or hinted at. In his 1780 *Collection* John divided the poem into three hymns, Nos. 225, 226, and 227. Dr Julian, in his standard *Dictionary of Hymnology*, noted, 'This hymn is sometimes ascribed to John Wesley, but upon what authority we have been unable to ascertain.' According to C.D. Hardcastle (W.H.S. *Proceedings*, II.200) it was because the hymn was 'supposed to be of a more classic character and statelier diction than those written by Charles'. This rightly questioned tradition must surely receive strong confirmation when we discover that the poem contains three complete lines which correspond exactly — in one case almost exactly — with lines in three other hymns which are almost certainly written by John, being his undoubted translations from the German. All may be seen in the *Collection*: 'And glory ends what grace begun' (226:8, see 188:24, which had 'end', not 'ends'); 'Before the world's foundation slain' (227:2 see 182:4); and 'The power omnipotent is thine' (227:22 see 232:46). Of course this cannot be regarded as absolute proof of John's authorship, but it is as near as makes little difference.

Theological and temperamental differences between the two brothers were undoubtedly exacerbated in the 1760s, but many of them had already been present in Charles's two 1749 volumes of *Hymns and Sacred Poems*. Indeed similar peculiarities in their approach to the doctrine of Christian perfection were present during the earlier years, when John (apparently) had penned the three prefaces to their joint volumes of *Hymns and Sacred Poems*, of 1739, 1740, and 1742, each of which emphasized this theme. John had accepted into the volumes a number of hymns by his brother about which he had some reservations. These reservations eventually emerged as marginal comments in his own copies, especially as they were being prepared for new editions. One major textual clue to authorship may be that while *literary* revisions were frequently made by John in his own writings, *doctrinal* revisions in jointly sponsored text usually indicated his brother's authorship of that text. In his *Plain Account of Christian Perfection* (1766), John deliberately sought to tone down the 'strongest account' of Christian perfection he had ever given, that in the 1740 preface.[2] Their joint acceptance of the doctrine in 1740 had been exemplified in the hymn, 'Lord, I believe a rest remains', which ended, 'Let all I am be God.' In 1766 John moderated this mystical phrase to 'Let all be lost in God,' which he followed also in his 1780 *Collection* (No. 391). John never mentioned the individual responsibility for the hymn, of course, but his changes in and omissions from it, both in 1766 and 1780, make it quite clear that the author must indeed have been Charles. The original version contained other examples of Charles's overstating his case, especially in stanzas 4 and 5 (omitted by John in 1766 and 1780): 'We wrestle not with flesh and blood, / We *strive* with sin no more', and 'We cannot, no, we cannot sin, / For we are born of God', which itself was a 1743 revision of the text of the first edition, 'We cannot now, we cannot sin.'

Undoubtedly the differing viewpoints of the two brothers may furnish valuable indicators of their authorship. Of even more importance may be their style, and especially their vocabulary. There is no question that Charles's writing tended to be exuberant and unrestrained, while John's was severe and sober. John's abhorrence of sentimentality and endearments is a very important ingredient in assessing his translations from the German. As Dr Nuelsen pointed out, John was an excellent translator, rarely taking the simple but dangerous course of sticking to the literal meaning, but striving to reproduce the basic thought of the original.[3] Frequently, however, he could not avoid words which were basically distasteful to him, such as 'blood' and 'wounds'. Sometimes the element of mysticism was so strongly present that it needed reproduction, in as mild a form as possible, or John would have to throw out the spiritual baby with the mystical bath-water. He did indeed totally reject some words which were erotic or ridiculously fanciful, as in the case of 'we kiss thy nail-holes'; similarly he changed 'kiss of faith' to 'arms of faith', and 'sweet mouth' to 'enlivening voice'.[4] Some of the more outrageous examples he pilloried in his *Hymns composed for the use of the Brethren* (1749).[5]

After the death of his brother Charles, John Wesley reverted to some of the problems of those early years, and pointed out publicly some distinctive features of his own writing and editing as opposed to that of the Moravians and of his brother. This was in his sermon, 'On Knowing Christ after the Flesh' (1789), where he devoted four paragraphs to this theme.[6] In §7, without naming him, he complained about the 'coarse expressions' which appeared in many of Zindendorf's 'truly spiritual hymns', so that 'often in the midst of excellent verses are lines inserted which disgrace those that precede and follow.' In §8 he stated that in translating German hymns he 'particularly endeavoured, in all the hymns ...addressed to our blessed Lord, to avoid every *fondling* expression.' In §9 he came to specific words and phrases: 'Some will probably think that I have been over-scrupulous with respect to one particular word, which I never use myself in verse or prose, in praying or preaching, and in giving thanks ...–"dear Lord", or "dear Saviour"', even though, he continued, 'my brother used the same in many of his hymns, even as long as he lived.' In §10 he warned against ever using such unscriptural expressions about our Lord even in private conversation, and confessed: 'I have sometimes almost scrupled singing (even in the midst of my brother's excellent hymn), "That dear, disfigured face", or that glowing expression, "Drop thy warm blood upon my heart."' Strangely enough he had retained those very lines in *Collection* 124:20 and 179:21, together with (in 179) the line following, 'And melt it by thy dying love.'[7]

John Wesley leaves it quite clear, however, that although he felt it necessary on occasion to quote some of his brother's phrases — just as he had quoted some Moravian expressions — this was not the kind of language that he himself would originate. Wherever unduly amorous terminology is applied to God in a hymn supposedly written by John, it should arouse immediate suspicion. 'Melt, happy soul, in Jesu's blood', for instance, is questionable both from the thought and the vocabulary: neither 'melt' nor 'blood' are otherwise known in John's undoubted hymns.[8]

The actual agreement between John and Charles Wesley not to identify the individual components of their joint publications must surely have been made before March 1739, when the first volume of *Hymns and Sacred Poems* was published. The undertaking came to an undisputed end during the winter of 1748–49, when Charles began preparing to add two further volumes to the three which had already appeared under that same title. These contained only his own original compositions, and were published to demonstrate to her anxious parents his ability to support Sarah Gwynne as his wife, a demonstration backed up by John Wesley's guarantee that Charles's literary earnings would never fall below a hundred pounds per annum.[9] Long before that time, however, as we have seen, Charles had been publishing hymns on his own account, as well as having them incorporated in the prose works of his brother. Indeed, the evidence quoted above shows that before 1749 John and Charles had each published two extant poetical works under their own names, and Charles was undoubtedly responsible for twenty-four of the anonymous poetical works, against three by John.

Actually there is a plethora of evidence about some thousands of Charles Wesley's poetical output. Huge masses of verse are extant in his handwriting, sometimes in two or three different stages of composition, showing both revisions and subsequent revisions.[10] There are sufficient external clues for us to be fairly certain that almost every anonymous verse publication was by Charles. Apart from the interwoven clues contained in the journals and correspondence of both brothers, there can be little doubt, for instance, that the two pamphlets entitled *Hymns on God's Everlasting Love* (1741) were written and published by Charles: on 2 June 1741, Howell Harris recounted 'reading Chas. Wesley's Hymns on God's Decrees, and Universal Redemption, most dreadfully positive'.[11] Evidence of a different kind exists for another very popular hymn-pamphlet by Charles Wesley. John Wesley wrote to Charles in 1761: 'Pray tell R. Sheen I am hugely displeased at his reprinting the Nativity Hymns and omitting the very best hymn in the collection, "All glory to God in the sky, &c." I beg they may never more be printed without it. Omit one or two, and I will thank you. They are *Namby-Pambical*.'[12] It can hardly be doubted that John Wesley had no responsibility either for writing or publishing *Hymns for the Nativity of our Lord* in 1745, or for its vanished predecessors recorded only in William Strahan's printing ledgers for December 1743 and 1744! Nor, indeed, for most of the other broadsides or hymn-pamphlets on different seasons of the Christian year.

We are still left, however, with those five hundred hymns published under their joint names in the *Hymns and Sacred Poems* of 1739, 1740, and 1742, the *Collection of Psalms and Hymns* of 1743, pp. 206–88 of Vol. 3 of the *Collection of Moral and Sacred Poems* (1744), *Hymns on the Lord's Supper* of 1745, and *Hymns of Petition and Thanksgiving* of 1746. There is little doubt that most of the *selections* later made

from these volumes were prepared by John, with the undoubted exception of those chosen for *Hymns for those to
whom Christ is all in all* (1761). Almost all the subsequent
original volumes, however, were the work of Charles,
whether they bore his name on the title-page or not. In
spite of John's influence as editor of his brother's verse,
with its crowning success in the 1780 *Collection*, Charles
Wesley's creative achievements in the field of religious
verse, like his contemporary publishing activities, remain
immensely superior as well as more extensive. There is
little more that we can now do about determining the
individual responsibility for the first jointly published five
hundred hymns, however, other than applying to single
poems or small groups any clues possible which offer
some slight hopes. It appears certain that the firm assign-
ment of authorship to all of them can never be expected,
even though some features of the problem are gradually
becoming clearer.

In an appendix to his first edition of *The Hymns of
Methodism* (1913) Henry Bett made the bold experiment of
attempting to isolate the known compositions of John
Wesley and to compare these with Charles's undoubted
Hymns and Sacred Poems of 1749. Thus he tried 'to establish
certain canons that may serve to identify some other of the
hymns as his'.[13] He described six criteria, by the application
of which he deduced that eleven hymns in the 1780 *Collection*, in addition to the translations from the German,
might 'be confidently attributed' to John. This method he
extended in subsequent research, so that in the third
edition of 1945 he listed fifteen criteria for John's
work, and extended those probably written by him from
eleven to sixteen, including 'And can it be that I should
gain'.

Bett's canons were carefully summarized by Dr Beckerlegge in his introduction to the 1780 *Collection*:

1. A preference for simpler measures.
2. A preference for consecutive rather than alternate rhyming, i.e. *aabb* rather than *abab*.
3. A tendency towards a caesura in his octosyllabic lines.
4. A tendency towards elaboration and repetition of a thought.
5. A fondness for parallel expressions at the beginning of consecutive lines.
6. Use of enjambment, with the thought ending early in the second line.
7. The repetition of the first verse, either exactly or very little altered, at the close of the hymn.
8. A number of favourite words, such as 'duteous', 'dauntless', 'boundless'.
9. Very little, if any, use of compounds made up of a noun together with a past or present participle, and little use of compounds beginning 'all-'.
10. Few polysyllabic words, such as Charles delighted in.
11. The use of the prefix 'un-', while Charles preferred 'in-'.
12. The fondness for triads of nouns or verbs.
13. What Dr Bett called 'a certain stiffness of movement'.
14. The use of formal eighteenth-century phrases.
15. The use of such abbreviations as 'I'll', 'I'd'.[14]

It will be noted, of course, that none of these 'canons' are anything like proofs, but deal with *tendencies*, some having greater relevance and force than others, while several concurrent examples acquire cumulative significance. About some criteria doubts have been raised, and some additional suggestions have been made. I personally would strongly endorse the importance of Dr Bett's observation that John Wesley tended to arrange poems from different authors in blocks rather than singly. I would also extend the definition of No. 1, 'simple measures', to 'simple short iambic measures', for John seems rarely to have written stanzas of more than eight lines, nor after his youth to have dabbled in anapaestic or mixed metres, and rarely with trochaic.[15]

About the evidential base for testing Charles's poems there can be little doubt, though it would be desirable to extend it greatly (especially backwards, to isolate those with proven origins from the 1739–45 period), so as to secure a more definitive summary of his own early 'tendencies'. The evidential base for John's work should also be extended, especially by the inclusion of the forty-one adaptations from the poems of George Herbert which were completely reshaped, where he seems to have had no competition from Charles. His use of a Latinism is seen in 'Praise', where to make it singable John altered Herbert's 'I will move thee' to 'Incessant will I move.' Their evidence, as summarized by Canon F. E. Hutchinson, incontrovertibly supports some of the points made above. In order to transform Herbert's free verse into hymns John Wesley nearly always presented them in iambic verse, and even did this for all but two of the seven which Herbert had written in trochaic metres.[16]

On the other hand it is clear that we cannot accept without demur the assumption that Charles Wesley never translated from the German. True, John Wesley stated in 1789 that when he and Charles were on the voyage to Georgia with the Moravians, 'I translated many of their hymns', but he preceded this phrase with, 'we conversed with them',[17] so that Charles was at least a potential translater. Whitefield's letter to Charles of 30 December 1736, remarked 'All friends like the German hymn admirably', which seems to assume not only that the hymn was dispatched by Charles, but also translated by him.[18] Once this warning has enabled us to set aside a long-established tradition, we may be able to view other evidence more objectively.

In *A Collection of Moral and Sacred Poems* (1744) there is a pair of hymns given as Parts I and II of 'The Life of Faith'. Each of these is headed in one of Charles Wesley's manuscript collections as 'From the German', each is paraphrased from the 1737 *Gesangbuch*, each is annotated in his hand, and each later appears in Charles's *Hymns for those to whom Christ is all in all* (1761).[19] It would surely be folly to claim that these must have been translated by John, especially when the first, 'O how happy am I here', is in a trochaic metre, and the second, 'Melt, happy soul, in Jesu's blood', is one of those 'blood and wounds' hymns so disliked by John, even having 'blut und wunden' in its first German line!

One of the hymns translated from the German finds its focal problem in prosody. In *Hymns and Sacred Poems* of 1739 there is a group of three poems (pp. 107–13), clearly related by their subject matter, entitled 'Hymn of Thanksgiving to God the Father', 'Hymn to the Son', and 'Hymn to the Holy Ghost', each of which later appeared in Charles Wesley's 1761 collection. This group must surely be attributed to Charles, for he made great use of its peculiar mixed metre of a rhyming pair of iambic sixes followed by four cross-rhyming trochaic sevens.[20] These three hymns, however, follow the same mixed metre as 'Thou, Jesu, art our King', in the 1738 *Collection* (pp. 36–38), which was translated from Scheffler's 'Dich, Jesu, loben wir', and this itself represents the only German example in the *Gesangbuch* of that same unusual metre.[21] Did John himself actually prepare this translation, and do so in a mixed metre which later so attracted Charles that he immediately began to imitate it? On balance this seems at least probable, especially as its joints creak somewhat compared with the smoothly moving trilogy prepared in 1739 by the admitted prosodical expert, Charles. It does seem barely possible, however, that this was not simply a lone effort by John, but that Charles might also have tried his hand at it in Georgia, or even after his return from England, before he had learned to sing a new song on 21 May 1738. (Its addition after that date seems quite impossible in view of the fact that William Bowyer entered in his ledger the printing charges for that *Collection* — through John's agent James Hutton — on 24 May 1738.)

This constitutes another reminder that in trying to differentiate between the deliberately concealed authorship of John and Charles we are still dealing too frequently with tendencies, with possibilities and probabilities, with circumstantial evidence rather than with inescapable facts. When all the characteristics of the two brothers are compared, their patterns and proven examples of publishing, their personal tensions, theological, literary, and ecclesiastical differences, their prosodical peculiarities, we return with increased puzzlement to John's own statement that only 'a small part' of the 1780 *Collection* was by him — which may fairly be extended to a similar fraction of the huge Wesley corpus as a whole. It is more of an approximate calculation than a guess to claim that John Wesley's contribution to the hymns published from 1739 to 1746, even including the translations and the major revisions of other authors, was few if any more than a hundred, and that although we may achieve a reasonable likelihood about the authorship of some, about a handful we may remain for ever in doubt.[22]

Even the application of Bett's principles, important as they are, have lifted only a tiny corner of the veil. I have tabulated the findings of three massive searches by three careful scholars over eighty years, and the results merit study in order to assess the value of this method of determining the jointly-published poems which can (in Bett's phrase) 'be confidently attributed' to John. Bett himself

listed sixteen, Edward Houghton thirteen, and Oliver
Beckerlegge seven, or possibly eight.[23] Here we have a
total of twenty-three hymns, all but four of them in the
1780 *Collection*. Of these there is unanimous support for
two only, Nos. 264 and 341 in the *Collection*. For twelve
there is only one clear vote. These are meagre and dis-
appointing results, caused not through insufficient research,
I believe, but because of the difficulty of balancing the
weight of one piece of evidence against that of another,
and the scarcity of primary historical and textual facts
which can be set over against even a dozen slender
prosodical clues.

I believe that research is still both needed and practic-
able, however, which may well enable us to identify along
similar lines other undoubted contributions of John Wesley,
which may be counted in two digits, but not in three. And
it seems to me that there are some rules of thumb to be
observed before we embark on any further prosodical
research.

1. In testing the hymns for the characteristics of John
Wesley's verse it is absolutely essential to go back to the
original complete texts of a poem, never to depend upon
those selections clearly made by John Wesley himself, in
which he had already omitted stanzas or altered words.
(This, of course, includes the 1780 *Collection*.)

2. The testing should be restricted to those seven publications which are clearly designated as the joint work of
both brothers (see p. 108 above).

3. It seems wise to ignore any poems in *Hymns on God's
Everlasting Love* (1741) and *Hymns for those that seek
...Redemption* (1747), both of which were almost certainly
prepared and published by Charles alone.

4. Eliminate any poems which bear MS revisions in the
hand of Charles.

5. Eliminate any poems where any edition contains
doctrinal revisions in the hand of John.

6. Treat with strong suspicion any poems which contain, in any stanzas, phrases such as 'dear Lord', 'dear Saviour' or any 'fondling expression'.

7. Only after these precautionary measures have been taken (in my view) is it really worth while carrying out any prosodical researches on the residual texts which *may* be by John Wesley.

It is interesting to note that even Edward Houghton, one of Bett's strongest supporters, seems — after all the technicalities — to place his major emphasis upon the subject matter and the general 'feel' of a poem, an aesthetic and emotional reaction which may well negate all the prosodical evidence. Even while making a strong case for John's authorship of 'And can it be', he records similar techniques used in one of Charles's hymns in his favourite 6 6.7.7.7.7 mixed metre, and quotes it from *Collection* 145, adding memorable words: 'But [this] could not have been John's. It has verve, passion, nervous tension, a holy boldness before God — all in the vivid present of experience. John's style is altogether slower and heavier.' This, therefore, not the heaping up of technicalities, is the key to distinguishing between John and Charles. Houghton responds to Beckerlegge's challenge that Charles's poetry 'soars' that a jumbo-jet also soars, as occasionally does John's verse, but in doing so it remains slower and heavier'. And this, it seems, when all is said and done, is the main point of distinction between Charles and John.[24]

In the index to *Hymns and Psalms*, under the name of Charles Wesley, is a symbol marking eight of his hymns, with the note: 'The authorship of these hymns is in dispute. They may be the work of John Wesley. The discussion regarding the authorship of the Wesley corpus is continuing, and the present index should not be taken as a final word on the issue.'[25] Many other words will be written in addition to these in 1983 and in 1988, but it is doubtful whether there can be any final word.

15

Conclusion

Poetry is sometimes described as the compromise between
the demands of a regular adherence to a metrical form
and the opposing urge of a mind fired by strong emotions.
True poetry is the result of extreme tension. Without the
discipline of metre the emotion might be expressed in
lyrical prose; without the emotion it would remain an
exercise in verse.

In the verse of Charles Wesley at his best we see the
happiest results of this tension. On the one hand there is
the classical restraint, the chaste, often sombre diction,
strangely allied with the artificiality of the rhetorician's
stock-in-trade. On the other there is the wide range of
deep and high emotions, covering the realms of the family
and public life, but at their most intense in the alternating
longings, despairs, and raptures of the soul's contact with
God. These emotions burst the fetters of conventional
verse, demanding expression in a rich and daring variety
of lyrical forms.

It is true of Wesley as of Wordsworth that his reputation
has suffered because he allowed much of his weaker writing to survive. With him a live metaphor sometimes
degenerates into a dead cliché; he is guilty of many flat
lines, many clumsy, a few maudlin. John Wesley's pungent
criticism of his brother's often-corrected manuscript
hymns on the Gospels and the Acts applies to his work as a

whole: 'Some are bad, some mean, some most excellently good', though it should be noted that 'mean' signified 'average'. My final word, however, must be to echo John Wesley's considered tribute to the spirit of poetry breathing through his brother's verse, even though he rated this as second in importance to the spirit of piety: 'Lastly, I desire men of taste to judge — these are the only competent judges — whether there is not in some of the following verses the true spirit of poetry, such as cannot be acquired by art and labour, but must be the gift of nature.'[1]

NOTES

1 *The Discovery of Charles Wesley*

1. *Dictionary of National Biography*, article 'Charles Wesley'.
2. *The Hymns of Wesley and Watts*, 1942, p. 14.
3. Preface to the 1780 *Collection*, §6.
4. *History of Eighteenth Century Literature*, 1891, p. 230.
5. *History of English Poetry*, Vol. V, 1905, p. 343.
6. *History of English Prosody*, Vol. II, 1923, p. 501; cf. pp. 507, 530–1.
7. *Survey of English Literature, 1730–1780*, Vol. II, 1928, pp. 224–6.

2 *Charles Wesley's Literary Output*

1. *History of English Prosody*, Vol. II, 1923, p. 531.
2. See *Rep. Verse*, 185, 187, 195; cf. 240 and 254, the former left permanently unfinished, the latter an 'imperfect hymn just as it came to [his] mind', later revised for publication.
3. Moore's footnote translates: 'The man is mad, or making verses.'
4. Ie. Wesley's House adjoining Wesley's Chapel, City Road, London.
5. Vol. II, 1825, pp. 368–9.

3 *Classical Training*

1. Moore's *John Wesley*, Vol. II, pp. 366–7. For examples and a discussion see *Rep. Verse*, 232–3
2. See *Rep. Verse*, 292, 302, 310–11.

4 *The Spiritual Impetus*

1. J. E. Rattenbury, *The Evangelical Doctrines of Charles Wesley's Hymns*, 1941, pp. 59–60.
2. See G. H. Findlay, *Christ's Standard Bearer*, 1956, pp. 67–74.
3. J. E. Rattenbury, *The Evangelical Doctrines of Charles Wesley's*

Hymns, 1941, pp. 28–31; T. S. Gregory, article on 'Charles Wesley's Hymns and Poems' in the *London Quarterly Review*, Vol. 182, 1957, pp. 253–62. This same identification with the deepest spiritual experience of every man is one of the reasons why Charles Wesley's verse can be so effectively used in private devotions. The cover of Dr J. Alan Kay's *Wesley's Prayers and Praises*, 1958, an anthology of lesser-known poems for devotional use, claims that Wesley 'speaks to our condition with a directness which is without parallel'.

5 *Charles Wesley's Vocabulary*

1. *Purity of Diction in English Verse*, 1952, pp. 76–7.
2. *The Hymns of Methodism*, 1945, pp. 35–46. (Originally published in 1913 as *The Hymns of Methodism in their literary relations*, enlarged in 1920, and greatly enlarged as well as recast for the third edition in 1945, with its shorter title – henceforth *Hymns* only.)
3. *Christ's Standard Bearer*, p. 16.
4. 'Where shall my wond'ring soul begin': 'antepast', a foretaste.
5. 'Arm of the Lord, awake, awake!': 'disparted', dividing in two, like the Red Sea for the children of Israel, about whom he has been writing.
6. 'Let earth and heaven combine': 'latent', concealed. This may be a reminiscence of St Thomas Aquinas, whose hymn *Adoro te devote* speaks of 'latens Deitas'. See Bett, *Hymns*, pp. 112–14.
7. 'All praise to our redeeming Lord': 'concentred', having a common centre.
8. For fuller details of Charles Wesley's use of the Greek NT see Bett, *Hymns*, pp. 81–92; cf. *Collection*, pp. 162–3.
9. 'Sovereign, everlasting Lord', in *Collection of Psalms and Hymns*, 1743, pp. 66–7. In the 3rd (1744) and later editions Wesley found it desirable to add the following footnote to 'little less than God': 'So it is in the Hebrew.' For these and other references to Wesley's use of the Hebrew see Bett, *Hymns*, pp. 76–8. It should be noted that Wesley's approach to the Hebrew text was strongly influenced by Matthew Henry's commentary; see Rev. A. Kingsley Lloyd's article, 'Charles Wesley's debt to Matthew Henry', in the *London Quarterly Review*, Vol. 171, 1946, p. 333.

10. Cf. Manning, *The Hymns of Wesley and Watts*, pp. 24–6. For a study of Charles Wesley's use of the verbs 'feel' and 'prove' see Findlay, *Christ's Standard Bearer*, pp. 39–46.

11. Cf. Bett, *Hymns*, pp. 35–49; G. H. Vallins, *The Wesleys and the English Language*, 1957, pp. 21–4, 70–4.

12. Bett, *Hymns*, p. 34.

13. *Short Hymns on Select Passages of the Holy Scriptures*, 1762, Vol. 2, p. 430, henceforth noted as *Scripture Hymns*. Cf. *Collection*, 76.

14. Bailey's *Dictionary*, 15th edn, 1753.

15. His original coining has happily been restored in *Hymns and Psalms*, 719 (ii).

16. *Rep. Verse*, p. 132.

17. *Rep. Verse*, p. 282; cf. *Poetical Works*, IX. 180.

18. O. A. Beckerlegge, 'Charles Wesley's Vocabulary', *London Quarterly Review*, April 1968, pp. 152–61.

19. I am indebted to Dr George W. Williams of Duke University for pointing out Wesley's indebtedness here to Pope's *Essay on Criticism*, lines 346–7:

> While expletives their feeble aid do join,
> And ten low words oft creep in one dull line.

Pope, in his turn, was adapting a passage in Dryden's *Essay on Dramatic Poetry*.

6   *Literary Allusions*

1. For these poems see *Rep. Verse*, 40, 127, and Bett, *Hymns*, pp. 124–9, 163–8.

2. *Hymns*, pp. 130–69. Cf. also Davie, *Purity of Diction*, pp. 73–5, and *Collection*, pp. 38–44, James Dale's 'The Literary Setting of Wesley's Hymns', emphasizing Miltonic allusions; see also General Index under 'allusions in hymns', with its list of twenty-three specific poets.

3. Vol. 1, pp. 91–192.

4. Letter of 1 October 1778, where his request that she should begin by memorizing Book I must be read against the background of his commendation of Miss Morgan's example, who, in following his plan of study, 'has got a good part of Prior's Solomon by heart' (*Journal*, Vol. 2, pp. 278, 280.)

5. Bett, *Hymns*, pp. 151–5, especially p. 153.

6. I am indebted to the Rev. A. S. Holbrook for pointing out that Jeremy Taylor's *Holy Dying* uses the phrase 'contract Divinity into a span'.

7. The Wesleys exerted a great though often indirect pressure towards wider literacy, for converts wanted to be able to read their Bibles and their hymn-books.

8. From his 'Hymn to the Holy Ghost', *Hymns and Sacred Poems*, 1739, pp. 111–13. See *Rep. Verse*, pp. 7–9.

9. Bett, *Hymns*, pp. 94–7: Mr Lloyd's article in the *London Quarterly Review*, Vol. 171 (1946), pp. 330–7, is noted above. Dr Routley's article was first published in Bulletin 69 of the Hymn Society (Autumn, 1954), pp. 193–9, and reprinted in the *Congregational Quarterly* for October, 1955, pp. 345–51. See also *Collection*, notes on pp. 251–2, 356, 381–3, 465, 472, 474, 667.

10. *Hymns*, pp. 98–123.

11. *Proceedings* of the Wesley Historical Society, I. 26–7.

12. Rattenbury, *The Evangelical Doctrines of Charles Wesley's Hymns*, pp. 47–52, especially p. 48. Cf. Bett, *Hymns*, pp. 71–97; Manning, *The Hymns of Wesley and Watts*, pp. 37–42; Davie, *Purity of Diction in English Verse*, p. 73; see also John W. Waterhouse, *The Bible in Charles Wesley's Hymns*, 1954.

7   *The Art of Rhetoric*

1. *Hymns for the use of families*, 1767, No. 124: *Poetical Works*, VII. 149. See *Rep. Verse*, p. 148.

2. 'Let earth and heaven combine' from the *Nativity Hymns*, No. 5: *Poetical Works*, IV. 109–10.

3. This is the opening quatrain and stanza 3, omitted from *Hymns and Psalms*, No. 109; see *Rep. Verse*, p. 57.

4. *Collection*, 48, pp. 139–40.

5. *Rep. Verse*, pp. 3–4; this is from stanza 6, omitted from Wesley's *Collection*, No. 29, as well as from modern hymn-books.

6. *Collection* 9:10, where a parallel in Milton is noted.

7. 'How happy are they', *Hymns and Sacred Poems*, 1749, I. 123–5: *Poetical Works*, IV. 409. See *Rep. Verse*, p. 103.

8. There is a similar construction in the closing two stanzas of 'Thou hidden Source of calm repose'. See also the second chapter of G. H. Findlay's *Christ's Standard Bearer*. This poem represents an interesting but by no means unique blend of evangelical urgency and devotional awe — the 'calmly-fervent

zeal' noted below (p. 44). It would certainly be possible, as pointed out by Dr E. M. Hodgson (*Proceedings* of the Wesley Historical Society, XXXVIII, 134–5, where the footnote relates to this work rather than to *Rep. Verse*) to sing the closing half 'slowly, as fitting the rhythm, and over five stanzas, each of which would form a convenient "stop" (like the close of a Beethoven concerto) ...' Indeed the *Collection* notes that the 'proffered benefits' of line 23 allude to the prayer after Communion's 'all other benefits of his Passion', which are spelt out in the following verses' (p. 92). And the tune *Invitation* to which it was set (p. 93) was indeed a somewhat heavily ornamented and stately two-four metre. Yet this is no quietly liturgical setting, even though it ends in 'speechless awe' and 'the silent heaven of love'. John Wesley placed it in the section 'exhorting, and beseeching to return to God', and the first half of the poem reaches a note of rapture: 'All heaven is ready to resound: / "The dead's alive, the lost is found!"'

9. 'And can it be, that I should gain', *Collection*, 193:13–16, with notes on the possibility of this being Charles Wesley's conversion hymn, on the kenosis doctrine here referred to, and an allusion to Alexander Pope.

10. See n. 5 above.

11. *Collection*, 47 (pp. 138–9, especially lines 3–4).

12. 'Jesu, Lover of my soul', see *Rep. Verse*, 15:27–8; cf. *Hymns and Psalms*, 528.

13. *Rep. Verse*, 91:13–15.

14. *Collection*, 61:19–24 (p. 157).

15. 'See the Day-spring from afar', *Rep. Verse*, 4:29–30 (p. 8).

16. *Hymns and Psalms*, 735:7–8.

17. 'Victim Divine, thy grace we claim', and 'God of unexampled grace', both from *Hymns on the Lord's Supper*; for the latter see *Rep. Verse*, 54:14, p. 73.

18. 'For a preacher of the gospel', in *Hymns and Sacred Poems*, 1740, from which was extracted the hymn 'Give me the faith which can remove', *Rep. Verse*, 78:20, p. 109.

19. 'All ye that pass by', *Rep. Verse*, 61:18, p. 83.

20. *Hymns and Psalms*, 101:15–16.

21. 'Thy causeless unexhausted love' from *Scripture Hymns*, I, 53–4 — altered to 'Thy ceaseless ...' in the 1780 *Collection*, 241:15–16.

22. 'O filial deity', *Collection*, 186:6, p. 313.

23. 'Hark, how all the welkin rings' — altered by George Whitefield to 'Hark, the herald angels sing', *Rep. Verse*, 8:25, p. 13.

24. 'Jesu, Lover of my soul', *Rep. Verse*, 15:5, p. 22.

25. *Rep. Verse*, 81:3–4, p. 113.

26. *Collection*, 193:1–6, p. 322.

27. 'Hear, Holy Spirit, hear', *Rep. Verse*, 51–2, p. 8.

28. *Collection*, 505:23–6, p. 696.

29. Findlay, *Christ's Standard Bearer*, pp. 38–9.

30. 'Hark, the herald angels sing', *Rep. Verse*, 8:132, p. 14.

31. 'Father, Son, and Holy Ghost', from *Hymns on the Lord's Supper*, see *Hymns and Psalms*, 791:2, and from 'Praise the Father for his love', from *Hymns for Children* (*Rep. Verse*, 108:6, p. 146).

32. *Rep. Verse*, 17:11–12, p. 24.

33. *Collection*, 27:6, 12, 18, 24, pp. 114–15.

34. See pp. 66–7 below.

35. Phil. 4.4.

36. *Rep. Verse*, 59:5–6, 35–6, and *Hymns and Psalms*, 243 (in five stanzas), set to Handel's tune, Gopsal. For a fuller study of the refrain in Wesley, by Oliver Beckerlegge, see *Collection*, pp. 51–4.

37. *Rep. Verse*, 17:16–20, p. 24. Cf. John Wesley's italicizing of the personal pronouns in his account of the warmed heart experience of 24 May 1738: 'an assurance was given me that he had taken away *my* sins, even *mine*, and saved *me* from the law of sin and death.'

38. *Rep. Verse*, 9:32–3, p. 15.

39. *Rep. Verse*, 15:13–14, p. 22.

40. *Rep. Verse*, 20:19–20, p. 30.

41. *Collection*, 367:6, p. 536.

42. *Rep. Verse*, 54:15–17, p. 73.

43. *Rep. Verse*, 63:36–42, p. 88.

44. *Rep. Verse*, 80:5–9, p. 111; cf. *Collection*, 324, p. 480, with two successful verbal revisions by John Wesley, as well as the omission of one stanza.

45. *Rep. Verse*, 22:31–2, 35, 40–6, 49–54, pp. 33–4; cf. *Collection*, 33, pp. 121–3, from which John Wesley has omitted stanza 6.

46. *Rep. Verse*, 58:13–24, pp. 78–9; cf. *Collection*, 418, p. 593, with some minor revisions by John Wesley.

8 Structure

1. See p. [48] above.

2. *Collection*, 466:11, p. 649.

3. 'Sing, ye ransomed nations sing', from *Nativity Hymns*, see *Rep. Verse*, 46:31–2, p. 64.

4. *Rep. Verse*, 61:21, p. 83.

5. *Rep. Verse*, 112:8, p. 149.

6. 'What shall I do my God to love', a hymn extracted from the poem 'After a recovery', *Hymns and Sacred Poems*, 1749, I. 162–4; see *Rep. Verse*, 74:39–40, p. 104.

7. *Collection*, 33:1–2, p. 121.

8. *Rep. Verse*, 15:29–32, p. 22. See Manning, *The Hymns of Wesley and Watts*, pp. 21–3, and cf. Findley, *Christ's Standard Bearer*, p. 32.

9. 'When our redeeming Lord', *Rep. Verse*, 31:36, p. 49.

10. 'Join all ye joyful nations', *Rep. Verse*, 40: 28–9, p. 59.

11. *Collection*, 184:1–6, p. 311.

12. *Hymns and Psalms*, 457.

13. *The Hymns of Wesley and Watts*, p. 69.

14. Ibid., pp. 39–40. See *Collection*, 209, and *Hymns and Psalms*, 781.

15. *Rep. Verse*, 80:37–40 (p. 12); cf. *Collection*, 324:31–6, p. 481, where it becomes stanza 6 after the omission of stanza 3.

16. *Collection*, 31:1–6, p. 119. This stanza begins a cento in common use until the *Methodist Hymnbook* of 1904; it comes from 'See, sinners, in the gospel glass', No. 10 in *Hymns on God's Everlasting Love*, 1741.

17. *Purity of Diction in English Verse*, pp. 72–3.

18. *Rep. Verse*, 255:59–60, p. 284.

19. *Rep. Verse*, 161:12, p. 211.

20. *Rep. Verse*, 170:22–4, p. 216.

21. *Rep. Verse*, 117:7–8, 15–16, 41–64.

22. R. Newton Flew, *The Hymns of Charles Wesley: a study of their structure*, 1953, pp. 21–5. See *Rep. Verse*, 74:41–72, pp. 104–5. Of the original poem of 72 lines *Collection* (207, pp. 338–9) included also at the beginning stanza 9 (lines 33–6, 'Infinite, unexhausted Love'), while *Hymns and Psalms* (46) omits both that and stanzas 16 and 18. In these days we prefer both our sermons and our hymns, as well as our hymn-sermons, somewhat shorter.

23. Findley, *Christ's Standard Bearer*, p. 37; see *Collection*, 137:29–32, p. 253. The original poem contained two further stanzas, but this sermon in miniature furnished a fitting close.

24. 'The Communion of Saints', Part I, *Hymns and Sacred Poems*, 1740, p. 188; see *Collection*, 501:9–16, p. 690.

25. *Rep. Verse*, 25:1–84, pp. 37–9. *Collection*, 136, pp. 250–2, omits stanzas 5 and 7, followed by *Hymns and Psalms*, 434.

9 *Metre*

1. *Representative Verse*, pp. 396–403. The first 'Attempt at a Classification of Charles Wesley's Metres' was made in a valuable article by the Rev. Dr O. A. Beckerlegge, in the *London Quarterly Review*, Vol. 169 (1944), pp. 219–27. To this I remain greatly indebted, even though fuller research has made it necessary to amplify, rearrange, and very occasionally correct, Dr Beckerlegge's pioneer study.

2. I am fairly confident that he also wrote 'Thee, O my God and king', although it has always been claimed for John Wesley, on the mistaken assumption that Charles never translated German Hymns. See *Rep. Verse*, pp. 4–5.

3. Cf. Dr Beckerlegge's notes on this in *Collection*, pp. 53–4. Mr Findlay has pointed out (*Christ's Standard Bearer*, p. 22) that this metre can be regarded as trochaic throughout by looking upon the iambic lines as a continuation of the trochaic lines; they would then be described as 13 13.7.7.13 and 13 13.15 13. The same is true of some other of the mixed metres. Nevertheless it seems clear that they were a different *genre*, certainly not to be explained as an accidental or prudential chopping up of a poem with over-lengthy lines.

4. For a discussion and a parallel presentation of Wesley's original and revised versions of this hymn, see *Rep. Verse*, 84, pp. 117–21.

5. Set out as 10 10.11 11. See *Rep. Verse*, 24, pp. 36–7.

6. Ibid., 335, pp. 367–8, with illustration facing p. 377.

10 *Modulations*

1. Called by Mr Findlay (*Christ's Standard Bearer*, pp. 25–6), a 'hammer-head'.

2. *Rep. Verse*, 30, pp. 45–8, *Collection*, 258–60, pp. 399–403, *Hymns and Psalms*, 719, each with different selections.

3. Sampson, *History*, p. 774.

4. There had been many others before him, of course, even among the hymn-writers — witness Bishop Thomas Ken's well-known Morning and Evening Hymns, and Watts's 'O God, our help in ages past'.

5. *Collection*, 2:33–4, p. 82.
6. *Hymns*, pp. 54–6.

11 *Rhymes*

1. *The Wesleys and the English Language*, 1957, p. 85; for some of his exemplars see pp. 81–4.

2. *Hymns*, pp. 50–6. The variations in accent were noted on the previous page.

3. *Collection*, 490:5–8, p. 677, and *Hymns and Psalms*, 773:5–8.

4. See further Chapter 8, 'Eighteenth-Century Language', in J. H. Whiteley's *Wesley's England*, especially pp. 232–7; cf. Bett, *Hymns*, pp. 47–9, G. H. Vallins, *The Wesleys and the English Language*, pp. 21–4, 50–68, and the poem of Dr Byrom's quoted in part by both Whiteley and Bett, which will be found in the *Gentleman's Magazine*, Vol. 28 (1758), p. 487.

5. *Rep. Verse*, 34:1–6, 'An Act of Devotion' appended to John Wesley's *A Farther Appeal*. He may have been responsible for a change from Charles Wesley's original manuscript, which apparently read 'guiding eye', from Ps. 32:8, in spite of the awkwardness of being guided by an eye. John changed it back in MS Colman, however, as Charles did in 1749 and 1761, so that 'eye' was used also in *Collection* (417:2), and thence eventually copied into *Hymns and Psalms*, 788.

6. *Collection*, 190:7–8, 11–12, pp. 319–20; cf. *Hymns and Psalms*, 569, where the fact that they are internal rhymes is obscured by the omission of the caesura.

7. *Rep. Verse*, 69, pp. 95–6; *Collection*, 374, and *Hymns and Psalms*, 267, both omit stanza 3, with 'Spirit/inherit' and the awkward masculine rhyme 'Omega be/liberty'.

8. *Rep. Verse*, 33: 2/5, 12/15, 17/20, 36/40, pp. 51–2. *Methodist Hymn-Book* (1933), 411, followed by *Hymns and Psalms*, 818, replaced stanza 3 (positioned as stanza 2) with a stanza from Charles Wesley's *Short Hymns on . . .Scripture* (II.67), so that their lines 17/20 have an eye-rhyme, 'discover/over'.

9. *Poetical Works*, IV.88.

10. See J. E. Rattenbury, *The Evangelical Doctrines of Charles Wesley's Hymns*, p. 53. Even the example of motes dancing in a sunbeam which Dr Rattenbury quotes as a visual word-picture was in fact taken direct from a German original, see *Rep. Verse*, pp. 170–2.

13   *The Study of the Wesleys' Hymns*

1. 'A Farther Account of the Rev. John Wesley, M.A.', p. 9, appended to Richard Rodda's *A discourse delivered ...March 13th, 1791, on occasion of the death of the Rev. John Wesley, A.M.*', Manchester, Radford, [1791].

2. Ibid., pp. 23–24.

3. *Collection*, p. 74.

4. John Hampson, *Memoirs of the late Rev. John Wesley*, Sunderland, 1791, 3 vols., III.157.

5. Robert Southey, *The Life of Wesley*, London, 2 vols, 1820, II.221–22.

6. Richard Watson, *The Life of the Rev. John Wesley*, 6th edn, London, Mason 1835, pp. 300–02.

7. Thomas Jackson, *Life of the Rev. Charles Wesley*, London, Mason, 2 vols, 1841, I.243.

8. David Creamer, *Methodist Hymnology*, New York, 1848, pp. 18–26, 84–92.

9. *The Poetical Works of John and Charles Wesley*, ed. G. Osborn, London, Wesleyan Methodist Conference Office, 13 vols., 1868–72, I.xiii.

10. Ibid., V.xi.

11. Ibid., VIII.xv–xvi.

12. Ibid., IX.viii–x.

13. Their early printer, William Strahan, seems to have been a little confused, and after heading their first page in his account book (July 1739 to May 1741) 'Mr. Charles Wesley Dr.', followed this up (August 1741-April 1742) with 'Mr. John Wesley & Br. Drs.', and then (April 1742-September 1743) with 'The Revd. Mr. John & Charles Wesley's Drs.'

14. See the 1761 numbers (with the *Collection* numbers in parentheses): 19 (444), 44 (403), 48 (199), 57–9 (225–7), 100 (427–8), while in the case of 97 (421) John simply omitted Charles's closing stanza.

15. Cf. John R. Tyson, *Charles Wesley on Sanctification*, Grand Rapids, Michigan, Francis Asbury Press 1986, pp. 248–61, etc.

16. Letters to Charles, June 27, July 9, 1766; cf. Tyson, op.cit., pp. 286–301.

17. *Sermons*, ed. A. C. Outler, 2:122–4; on this occasion John had given the credit — or assigned the responsibility — to Charles by name.

14   *The Major Problem: John or Charles?*

1. Cf. 'Thou hidden source of calm repose' (by Charles, *Collection*, 201:1) with 'O Jesu, source of calm repose', 343:1, presumably translated by John from a hymn by Freylinghausen. See also 'Fountain of unexhausted love', 328:2 and 163:13, the first (1739) possibly by John, the second (1741) certainly by Charles. See also 'Give him thanks, rejoice and sing', 189:43, 388:8; 'Give to mine eyes refreshing tears', 179:25, 202:31; 'Praise by all to thee be given' (again both brothers), 212:30, 340:31, and 419:5,35; 'Thee only would I know', 177:2, 341:36; 'What shall I do my God to love', 207:5, 367:1.

2. *Plain Account*, §§ 9, 13–16.

3. John L. Neulsen, D.D., *John Wesley and the German Hymn*, trans. Theo Parry, Sydney H. Moore, and A. S. Holbrook, Calverley, Yorkshire 1972, pp. 58–62.

4. Ibid., p. 56.

5. On pp. 6–7 he quotes from Hymn 57: 'Lovely side-hole, dearest side-hole, / Sweetest side-hole made for me, / O my most beloved side-hole, / I wish to be lost in thee.'

6. No. 123 in *Sermons*, Vol.4, ed. Outler, Abingdon Press, Nashville 1987.

7. Cf. John R. Tyson, 'Charles Wesley and the German Hymns', *The Hymn*, Vol. 35 (July 1984), pp. 156–7.

8. Cf. John R.Tyson, 'Charles Wesley's Sentimental Language', *Evangelical Quarterly*, Vol.57 (1985), pp. 269–75. Edward Houghton is surely exaggerating when he describes as characteristic of John's own writing the 'trace of sensuous German mysticism' and a love for the word 'wounds' ('John Wesley or Charles Wesley?', The Hymn Society of Great Britain and Ireland, *Bulletin* 146 (September 1979), pp. 96–7.

9. Frank Baker, *Charles Wesley as revealed by his letters*, Epworth Press 1948, pp. 63–65. I take this opportunity to point out that in this forty-year-old volume I made a serious historical *faux pas*. Receiving no replies to my suspicious letters of inquiry, I accepted as genuine a letter supposedly written by Charles Wesley to the wife of Oglethorpe, describing the supposed origin on Jekyl Island, Georgia, of 'the enclosed hymn . . .: Lo! on a narrow neck of land, / 'Twixt two unbounded seas, I stand' (p. 25), when in fact it was a literary hoax. Oglethorpe was not married until 1743. The forgery was prepared for reading to the Chicago Literary Club at its meeting in December 1892 by Franklin Harvey Head (1832–

1914), and privately printed 'for the amusement of his friends' in a four-page pamphlet, *Studies in Early American History, The Legends of Jekyl Island* ... Not surprisingly, it fooled others as well as me, including my source, John Telford, in his *Charles Wesley*.

10. For examples see *Rep. Verse*, facing p. 14, and the text of pp. 161–4, 168–72, for those of doubtful authorship; compare with these others obviously published by Charles, pp. 83, 142, 220–1, 224, 228. For the bulk of the Charles Wesley MS verse, see the same volume pp. 387–94; unfortunately one item was omitted from this list because it was kept in a separate strongbox containing items for exhibition, an octavo volume of almost two hundred pages, transcribed as a fair copy by Charles Wesley, which might be designated as the Pickard manuscript, from its former owner.

11. Tom Beynon, *Howell Harris's Visits to Pembrokeshire*, Cambrian News Press, Aberystwyth, 1966, p. 327.

12. Dec. 26, 1761, original holograph in Methodist Archives, Manchester. Though unnecessary, it should perhaps be pointed out that textual evidence also is available. In John's copy of the 4th edn of *Nativity Hymns*, Bristol, Farley, 1750, he changed 'sinless perfection' to 'spotless perfection' and 'dearest Lord' to 'gracious Lord' — see the copy in Methodist Archives, Manchester, pp. 18, 20.

13. Appendix IV, 'The Hymns of John Wesley', pp. 129–35.

14. *Collection*, pp. 35–6; cf. the fuller discussion, pp. 34–8.

15. Nuelsen, op. cit., pp. 108–62, shows that only one of the thirty-three German translations, No.1, 'O God, thou bottomless abyss', is larger than eight lines, and only two use trochaic measure, Nos. 6, 'Thou, Jesu, art our King', and 26, 'Holy Lamb, who thee receive'. (For No. 6 see below, n. 21.)

16. F. E. Hutchinson, 'John Wesley and George Herbert', *London Quarterly Review*, October 1736, pp. 439–55.

17. Sermon 123, 'On Knowing Christ after the Flesh', §8.

18. Luke H. Tyerman, *The Life of the Rev. George Whitefield*, 2nd edn, Hodder and Stoughton 1890, I.62. Cf. *Rep. Verse*, pp. 167–72, *Collection*, 34, 36–7, and John R. Tyson, 'Charles Wesley and the German Hymns', pp. 153–7.

19. *Rep. Verse*, pp. 168–72.

20. *Rep. Verse*, pp. 4–9. They begin, 'Thee, O my God and King', 'O filial Deity', and 'Hear, Holy Spirit, hear'.

21. Cf. n. 15 above.

22. Cf. Bett, *Hymns*, pp. 21–33; J.E. Rattenbury, *The Evangelical Doctrines of Charles Wesley's Hymns*, Epworth Press 1941, pp. 21–5, 58–84; Flew, *The Hymns of Charles Wesley*, pp. 26–31; *Collection*, pp. 34–8.

23. See Bett, *Hymns*, pp. 25–6; Edward Houghton, Bulletins 146, 155, 172, of the British Hymn Society (omitting the general listing on p. 237 of Bulletin 172, where no specific testimony is offered, and where the second part of '363/4' seems incorrect), and the 1780 *Collection*, p. 38.

24. Edward Houghton, 'John Wesley or Charles Wesley?', Bulletins 146 (pp. 94–5) and 172 (pp. 238–30).

25. *Hymns and Psalms*, p. cxxvii.

15   *Conclusion*

1. John Wesley, *Journal*, [23] December 1788; *Collection*, p. 74.

SELECT BIBLIOGRAPHY

I. Some collections of Charles Wesley's Verse.

The Poetical Works of John and Charles Wesley, ed. George Osborn, 13 vols., Wesleyan Methodist Conference Office 1868–72.

A Collection of Hymns for the Use of the People called Methodists. With a Supplement, Wesleyan Conference Office 1876. This is the largest collection, with a total of 1026 hymns, of which 724 are credited to Charles Wesley.

The Methodist Hymn-Book, Methodist Conference Office 1933, in which 243 of the 984 hymns are credited to Charles Wesley.

Hymns and Psalms. A Methodist and Ecumenical Hymn Book, Methodist Publishing House 1983, with 888 hymns and psalms, 173 by the Wesleys.

Representative Verse of Charles Wesley, ed. Frank Baker, Epworth Press 1962.

A Collection of Hymns for the Use of the People called Methodists, ed. Franz Hildebrandt and Oliver A. Beckerlegge, Vol. 7 in the Oxford / Bicentennial Edition of the Works of John Wesley, Clarendon Press 1983.

A Thousand Tongues: The Wesley Hymns as a guide to scriptural teaching, ed. John Lawson, Paternoster Press 1987.

II. Some studies of Charles Wesley's Verse.

Bett, Henry, *The Hymns of Methodism*, Epworth Press 1945.

Davie, Donald, *Purity of Diction in English Verse*, Chatto and Windus 1952. See especially chapter V, 'The Classicism of Charles Wesley'.

Findlay, George H., *Christ's Standard Bearer: a Study in the Hymns of Charles Wesley*, Epworth Press 1956.

Flew, R. Newton, *The Hymns of Charles Wesley: a Study of their Structure*, Epworth Press 1953. The Wesley Historical Society Lecture for 1953.

Hodges, H.A., and A.M. Allchin, *A Rapture of Praise: Hymns of John and Charles Wesley, selected, arranged, and introduced*, Hodder and Stoughton 1966.

Manning, Bernard L., *The Hymns of Wesley and Watts*, Epworth
    Press 1942.
Nuelsen, John L., *John Wesley and the German Hymn* (trans. Parry,
    Moore, Holbrook), A.S. Holbrook, Calverley, Yorkshire 1972.
Rattenbury, J. Ernest, *The Evangelical Doctrines of Charles Wesley's
    Hymns*, Epworth Press 1941.
—— *The Eucharistic Hymns of John and Charles Wesley*, Epworth
    Press 1948.

INDEX